Italian Folk Music For Mandolin

by John T. La Barbera

GW00505903

CD Contents

1	Addio Mia Bella Addio		16	La Fiera Di Mast`Andrea
2	Alla Renella		17	La Furlana
3	Amor Dammi Quel Fazzoletino		18	La Luna 'Nta Sta Ruga
4	Amore Mio Non Piangere (La Mondina)		19	La Manfredina
5	Ballo Tondo		20	La Monferrina
6	Bella Bimba-Varda Che Passa La Villanella		21	La Principessa Di Carini
7	Canto Di Cagliari		22	La Quadrighia
8	Cecilia		23	La Rotta
9	Cicerenella		24	La Serpe A Carolina
10	Curenta Della Val Chisone		25	La Veneziana
11	Danza Corale Ciclica Carnevalesca		26	La Vo`
12	Fateve `Nnanze		27	Michelemma`
13	Fenesta Vascia		28	Pizzica Tarantata
14	Festa A Taormina		29	Quel Mazzolin Di Fiori
15	I'Bambino `E Della Mamma		30	Re Gilardin

Online Audio Contents

1	Rumanele		6	Tarantella Spritusa
2	Schirazula Mirazula		7	Tutti Mi Dicon Maremma Maremma
3	Si Li Femmene Purtassero La Spada		8	Vieni Sul Mar
4	Tarantella Alla Montemarinese		9	Vilota Di Rovigo
5	Tarantella Calabrese		10	Vurria `Ca Fosse Ciaola

1 2 3 4 5 6 7 8 9 0

Visit us on the Web at www.melbay.com — E-mail us at email@melbay.com

Dedicated to the Loving Memory of Helen (Elena) La Barbera

Favorites of Italian Folk Music and Song For Mandolin

Compiled, Transcribed and Edited by John T. La Barbera
All arrangements by John T. La Barbera
Translations: Dr. Luisa Del Giudice and John T. La Barbera
Recording: John T. La Barbera: mandolin, mandola, chitarra battente, classical guitar, tamburello, and tricca-ballacca.

Table of Contents

Preface

This collection is a follow up to my first book, Traditional Southern Italian Mandolin and Fiddle Tunes. I was so pleased that the first collection had sparked much interest in Italian folk music through the mandolin, it seemed fitting to go further. The volume which you hold now, Italian Folk Music for Mandolin, delves deeply into the heart and soul of the music from the north to the central and southern regions of Italy, including the islands of Sicily and Sardinia. For this book, I have selected and transcribed 40 songs that variously include complete texts, translations, accompanying styles, additional parts for a second mandolin, violin or guitar, plus a recording of each song in the book. Above each piece, a brief description or background is included, giving the player a better understanding of the interpretation.

Italy is divided into 20 regions, from North to South. Although I did not cover all of the 20 regions, I tried to focus on some of the best examples of music from North, Central, and Southern Italy including Sicily and Sardinia. The music spans several centuries of both instrumental folk music and folk songs. My selections include medieval and renaissance instrumental dances, 16th Century Neapolitan Villanelle, work songs, lullabies, narrative ballads, historical songs, love songs, prisoner songs, and popular dances including: tarantella, pizzica, Sardinian ballo tondo, quadrille, waltz and saltarello.

I hope that this anthology of traditional Italian folk music and mandolin playing will be a valuable and enjoyable source for beginners, advanced players and vocalists, who desire to increase their repertoire of Italian songs. The music can be played either as instrumental pieces alone or as ensemble pieces with a vocalist. In trying to maintain a high standard of musical interest, I sincerely hope that other players will share the same enjoyment of discovering and playing this music as I have found.

John T. La Barbera

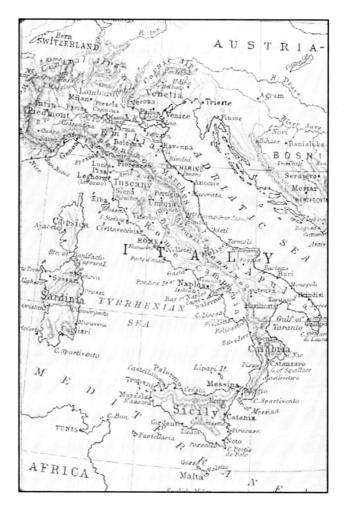

Introduction

Italy has long been known throughout the world for it's beloved melodies. From the grand opera, the arias of Verdi and Puccini to the famous Neapolitan classics of O Sole Mio, Torna Surriento, Finiculli Finiculla, etc., these songs have widely been accepted worldwide for well over one hundred years. On the other hand, Italian folk music, up until the late twentieth century, had remained basically regional and remote within the confines of its origins and had been passed down by oral traditions. The authors were all anonymous. As a result, it is common that one song may have hundreds of versions with variants in the melody or text. One basic fact is that Italian folklore remains distinctly regional. With profound differences in geography, history and language, the music expresses all of these qualities because it comes from the people who experienced it. The poetry of Southern Italy is lyric, while that of Northern Italy is narrative.

The melodies of the songs that I have selected for this book have the same beauty and intensity of the well-known music of Italy, but at the same time they represent the "genuine" folk music. One can clearly see the impact of Italian folk music on the art music and Neapolitan songs. For instance, *La Fiera de Mast'Andrea* has a comical character reminiscent of comic opera (opera buffa) of Rossini. The haunting melody in the ballad of "Cecilia" tells a tale similar to the tragedy in Puccini's Tosca. The song *Vieni Sul Mar*, considered to be a Neapolitan folk song (some accounts claim it to be a Venetian street ballad), was one of the first songs recorded in the early twentieth century by the world-famous tenor Enrico Caruso. Since then it has been an important staple of many tenors.

About The Music

The collecting and studying of Italian folk music dates back to the late nineteenth century where in Sicily, Giuseppe Pitre` (1841-1916), published two volumes called *Canti Popolari Siciliani* (1870-71). A folklorist, doctor and politician, Pitre` focused his attention on collecting the songs of the common people of Sicily. Pitre`'s valuable work describes the sentiment felt during this period regarding the preservation of traditional songs *"behind each song there is a poet, an individual imagination. Anonymously, the song passes from mouth to mouth, country to country over mountains and seas. In this journey, the song loses its author but finds it's singers, some who may alter the form or add to it, degrade it or improve it"*. In Southern Italian music, a connection to the traffic with other parts of the Mediterranean world can be heard, as in the *Tarantella alla Montemarinese*, or *Michelemma`."*

In Northern Italy, diplomat and author Costantino Nigra (1828-1907) called attention to the *epic lyric* songs from Piemonte in Northern Italy in his collection of songs called *Canti Popolari del Piemonte* (1888). One such song is *Re Gilardin*, from the Po Valley, is a tragic ballad that Italian scholars call *morte occulta* (occult death), belonging to the Gallo-Italic tradition. Derived from Celtic myth, its legend can be traced to other parts of Europe.

Included in the book are two Neapolitan villanelle from the 16th century; "Si Li Femmene Purtassero La Spada" ("If Women Carried Swords") and "Vurria `Ca Fosse Ciaola" *("I Wish To Become A Bird")*. The villanella originated from a style of folk poetry popular in rural areas, and always in the vernacular language. During the 16th century it was accompanied by tambourines and castanets. At that time in Naples, it had become a stylized form played to the accompaniment of the colascione, lute, guitar, mandola and the vielle. Trained musicians began to set the poetry to music, while keeping the essence of the earlier folk style. By the mid sixteenth century, two styles of villanelle emerged. One called popolaresca (folk-style), which had strong moral and social meanings; and the second type, dolce, was sweeter, a little meek and sentimental. All of the text had double meanings and in some instances was banned by the church. "Vurria `Ca Fosse Ciaola" is attributed to a popular character known for always being always short on money, who went by the nickname "Sbruffapappa." Folk poetry continued to be set to music with popular characteristics, as can be seen with the song "Fenseta Vascia," whose text can be traced to the 1500's, but the music is attributed to Guglielmo Cottreau in the mid-nineteenth century.

The mandolin has a long tradition in Italy as an instrument used in both art music and folk music. In Tuscany and Rome, stornelli were commonly played by street serenaders with guitar accompaniment. Stornelli were improvised poems structured in three-line verses, with brief instrumental improvisations played between the verses. The improvised texts generally gave voice to the lover pleading with the object of his affection. It soon became a customary part of the courtship ritual and is the origin of the image of musicians serenading a beloved under her balcony.

For The Mandolinist

This anthology offers a wide range of expression on the instrument and a chance for all musicians to expand their repertoire of Italian folk music. I have included an array of pieces of varying difficulty and length that are interesting and fun to play. For those who do not read music, all of the pieces are transcribed in tablature. There is no doubt that tablature is a simple and effective way to learn how to play songs, but it does have it's limitations. Listen closely to the accompanying recording for the rhythms of each piece, and try to follow the rhythms in the notated music. Standard notation is superior for communicating the harmony and the rhythm of the music. Having both types of notation at hand (no pun intended), can be advantageous. Throughout most of Italy, the mandolin is always accompanied by the guitar (or in Southern Italy, the chitarra battente), tambourine and castanets for both instrumental music and vocal music. It is common that the mandolin doubles the vocal lines, as I have notated.

Tremolo

The distinct Italian sound of playing sustained notes on the mandolin is known as *tremolo*. It is played by a rapid succession of down and up strokes, lasting the duration of the note value.

This idiomatic technique has always had popular appeal among folk musicians. It is rarely seen in written music from the seventeenth and eighteenth centuries, except as ornamentation. Even up until the nineteenth century, most written mandolin music was played single-stroke style. The preferred tremolo playing on even the shortest notes, once associated with Neapolitan street musicians, became known as the "cantabile tremolo style" or "singing tremolo style" which was always played legato. By 1835, the mandolin was fitted with high-tension steel strings, invented by Neapolitan luthier Pasquale Vinaccia. This further encouraged and enhanced the "cantabile style," and tremolo was used for everything as single-stroke playing fell out of style by the mid nineteenth century. Tortoiseshell plectrums replaced quill ones during this period, allowing mandolinists to produce a more robust and sustained tremolo. The mandolin always doubled the voice.

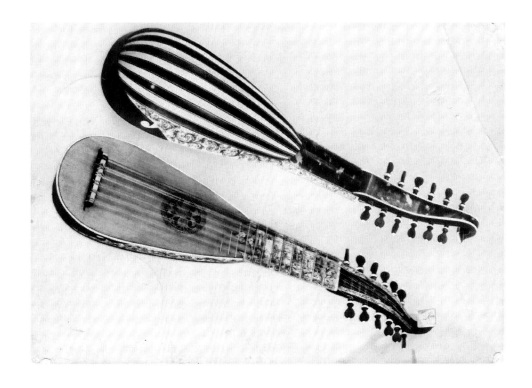

Rhythm For The Mandolinist and Guitarist

A distinguishing feature of this music is the variety in accompanying styles and rhythms used. Included are suggested rhythm patterns for both strumming and finger picking (for guitar), that can be used when playing in the traditional style. Once you are accustomed to the music, you will surely find your own variations based on these patterns.

The villanelle have their own unique form of accompaniment and are more stylized. There can be several meter changes within one piece, and the strumming should emphasize the rhythm of the melody. When finger picking, place your right hand fingers on the strings which your left hand is fretting, and follow the melodic rhythm when playing.

While following the strum patterns, pay close attention to the down and up symbols and where the accents fall. Remember, the accompaniment style is very important and enhances the melody; its the rhythm and accents that distinguish it as Italian folk music.

Battente Strumming

For the guitarist, strumming can be done with a pick or the with the right hand fingers. This type of strumming is derived from the renaissance Italian guitar called *chitarra battente*, a double course guitar with metal strings exclusively for strumming (it is still played in Southern Italy). It is purely a folk style that has evolved over the centuries and is similar to Flamenco guitar strumming and various folk styles from around the world, especially in Latin America.

When strumming without a pick, keep the index (i), middle (m), and ring (a) fingers close together as the hand brushes downward across the strings. For the up-strum, the hand moves up with only the thumb brushing across the strings, following the suggested strum pattern. There is also a slight variation of this technique in which the fingers of the right hand rotate in order, starting with the ring (a) followed by the middle (m) then the index (i) fingers creating a triplet pattern on the top three strings. This rotation in Calabria is called *rotuliata*.

Keeping Time

Musical time is measured in beats. Beats are organized into units called measures, which are divided by vertical lines called bar lines.

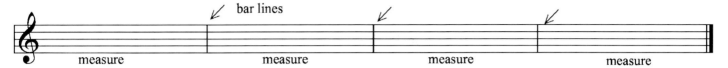

Meter

The most common meter is quadruple, with a strong accent appearing on the first beat, and a weaker accent on the third beat.

1 2 <u>3</u> 4 this is notated as 4/4 time.

Duple meter consists of two beats per measure, with the accents on the first beat.

1 2 **1** 2 this is notated as 2/4 time.

Triple meter consists of three beats per measure, with the accent on the first beat, and a weaker accent on the third beat.

1 2 <u>3</u> **1** 2 <u>3</u> this is notated as 3/4 time.

Time Signature

The time signature is placed at the beginning of each piece. The top number tells how many beats per measure, while the bottom number tells what kind of note receives one beat. These are known as Simple time signatures:

Compound Meter

Compound time signatures work differently. The top number represents the number of subdivisions there are in each measure. Most common in Italian music is 6/8, also 3/8, 9/8 and 12/8 time. These meters have a primary accent and a secondary accent. The beat is in multiples of 3. For example, divide the top number by 3 for the number of beats to the bar. In 6/8 time, dividing the top number (6) by three, equals two. Therefore we have two beats in a 6/8 measure.

1 2 3 4 5 6 = 6/8

1 2 3 4 5 6 7 8 9 = 9/8

1 2 3 4 5 6 7 8 9 10 11 12 = 12/8

The bottom number represents the note value that subdivides the beat. In 6/8 time, the 8 represents an eighth note, therefore three of them equal one beat.

3 eighths = one dotted quarter note to the bar

Time signature	Number of Beats	Type of Note that Gets the Beat
3/8	1	dotted quarter note
6/8	2	dotted quarter note
9/8	3	dotted quarter note
12/8	4	dotted quarter note

Subdivisions in Compound Time Signature

The chart below illustrates the subdivisions found in compound time. It works the same for all of the compound time signatures 3/8, 9/8 and 12/8. The dotted quarter note is subdivided into three eighth notes and each eighth note can be subdivided into two sixteenth notes. The counting of the subdivisions is indicated below.

Duplets are also common in compound time. An example of this is found in the *Tarantella Di Carnevale Alla Montemarinese*.

When following the strum and pick patterns, pay close attention to the subdivisions.

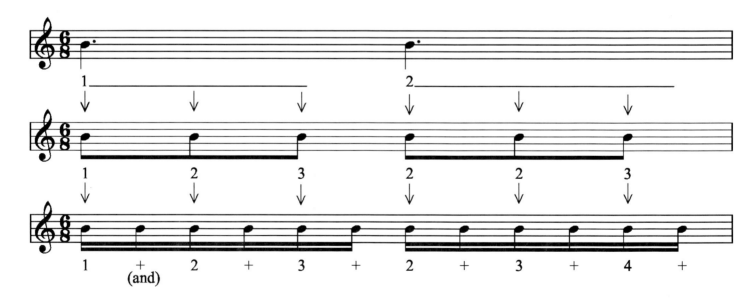

Duplets: Two notes in the space of three. It feels like two notes in simple time. The first duplet appears on the beat, the second one occurs on the + (and) of two.

Strum And Pick Patterns

The following strum and pick patterns are numbered according to the suggested patterns at the beginning of each song in this book. The picking patterns for the right hand below use the letters **p** (thumb), **i** (index), **m** (middle) and **a** (ring finger).

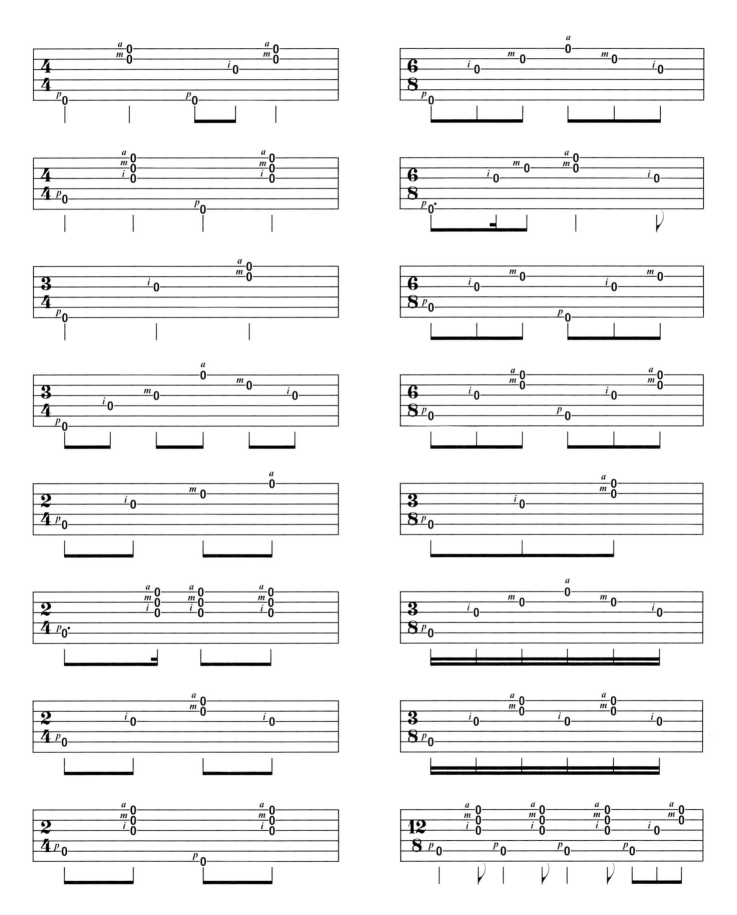

Italian Musical Expressions

Adagio – slowly, leisurely

Accelerando – gradually increasing speed

Allegretto – diminutive of allegro; moderately fast

Allegro – lively, brisk, rapid

Al Fine – to the end

Amoroso – affectionately

Andante – in moderately slow tempo

Andantino – diminutive of Andante, slower than Andante

A Piacere – at your pleasure

Arpeggio – broken chord, harp style

A tempo – in the original time

Barcarolle – a boatman's song, popular in Naples and Venice

Cantabile – in a singing style

Coda – a supplement at the end of the composition

Con Moto – with motion, animated

Da or dal – from

Da Capo (D.C.) – back to the beginning

Dal Segno (D.S.) – back to the sign

Fine – the end

Grave – very slow

Larghetto – slow, not as slow as Largo

Largo – broad and slow, the slowest tempo

Legato – smoothly, tied together

Maestoso – majestically, dignified

Meno Mosso – less quickly

Moderato – moderately

Mosso – equivalent to rapid

Piu` – more

Piu` Mosso – quicker

Presto – very quick

Prestissimo – as quick as possible

Rallentando (rall.) – gradually slower

Ritardando (rit.) – gradually slower and slower

Staccato – detached, separate

Tacit – silent

Tempo – movement, rate of speed

Tempo Primo – return to the original tempo

Troppo – too much

Veloce – quick, rapid

Vivace – with vivacity, bright, spirited

Vivo – lively

"Behind each song there is a poet, an individual imagination. Anonymously, the song passes from mouth to mouth, country to country over mountains and seas. In this journey, the song loses its author but finds it's singers, some who may alter the form or add to it, degrade it or improve it." G. Pitre`

Chord Dictionary

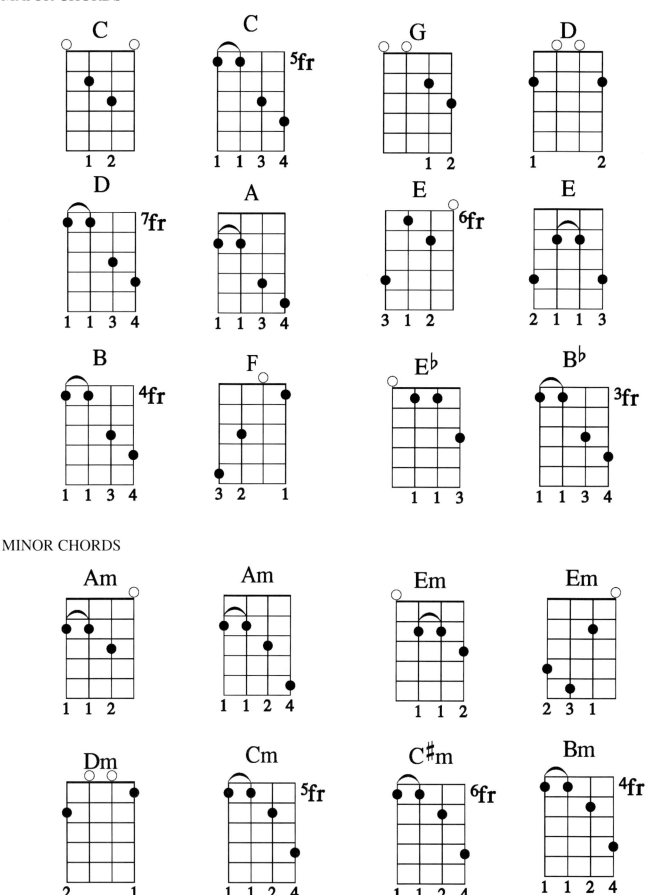

MAJOR CHORDS

MINOR CHORDS

MINOR CHORDS

Gm 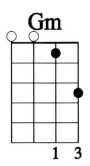 Gm⁶ 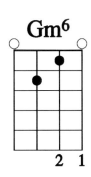 Fm 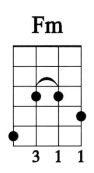 F#m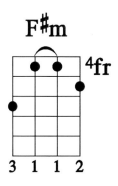

DOMINANT 7TH CHORDS

C⁷ 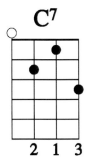 G⁷ 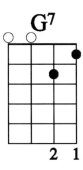 D⁷ 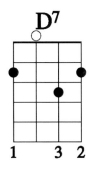 A⁷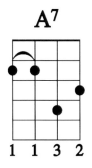

E⁷ 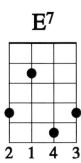 E⁷ 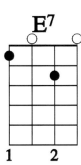 B⁷ 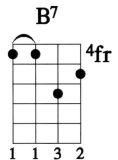 F⁷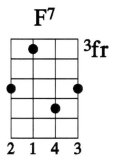

SUSPENDED CHORDS

E⁷ 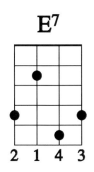 E⁷ 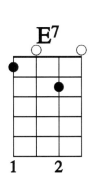 B⁷ 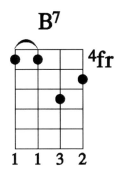 F⁷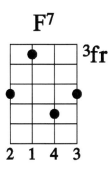

DIMINISHED CHORDS

Edim 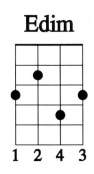 Fdim 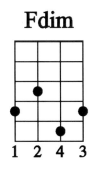 Fdim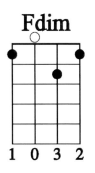

About the Author

Composer, arranger, guitarist, and mandolinist, **John T. La Barbera**, is the author of the first and foremost Italian mandolin book in the United States, *Tradional Southern Italian Mandolin and Fiddle Tunes*. The book is the first and foremost Italian mandolin book published in the United States by Mel Bay Publications and is one of their best sellers.

Awarded for his extraordinary role in the transmission and translation of Italian oral traditions from The Italian Oral History Institute, La Barbera is recognized as one of the first transcribers of Southern Italian folk music in America. Because of his expertise in Italian traditional music, La Barbera has been a valuable resource for directors of both film and theater.

Immediately after graduating with a Bachelor of Music degree in classical guitar from the Hartt School of Music in Hartford, Connecticut, he was awarded a scholarship to continue graduate studies in Siena and Florence, Italy. It was in Florence during the 1970's where John launched his professional career. He was selected as a full time guitarist and arranger for the folk music and theater company, *Pupi e Fresedde*, who honored his virtuosity and brought him acclaim in Italy and the rest of Europe. During those years, the group left an indelible mark with a tremendous contribution to Italian folk music, and was part of the first wave of the Italian folk music revival from that era. It was also during this time that he started to transcribe a huge repertoire of folk music that traditionally had been passed down by oral tradition. Upon his return to the U.S., he brought his experience and own transcriptions of this music back to form the group *I Giullari di Piazza*, in New York City in 1979.

As a composer, his film scores include the Academy Award Nominated feature documentary *Children of Fate*, (1992); *Sacco and Vanzetti* (2008), awarded best historical film from the American Historical Association; *Pane Amaro* (2008); *What's up Scarlet* (2005); *Neapolitan Heart–Cuore Napolitano* (2000); *La Festa* (1996) and *Tarantella* (1994).

In theater, he has worked as composer, arranger and musical director for several off-Broadway productions including Souls of Naples, starring John Turturro (Theater for a New Audience); Kaos, directed by choreographer Martha Clarke (New York Theater Workshop) for LaMaMa E.T.C., and has composed several fully staged folk operas including *Stabat Mater: Donna di Paradiso*; *The Voyage of the Black Madonna*; and *The Dance of the Ancient Spider*.

Recipient of several composing awards and commissions from The Jerome Foundation, Lincoln Center for the Performing Arts, The Martin Gruss Foundation, the New York State Council on the Arts, Meet the Composer, ASCAP and finalist in the Jazz category of the John Lennon Songwriting Competition.

Published works include *Traditional Southern Italian Mandolin and Fiddle Tunes*, Mel Bay Publications, 2009; *The MarimBaba Suite* for percussion quartet and *Danza del Fuego* for solo marimba, both published with Bachovich Music Publications, 2009; and has contributed a chapter in *"Oral History, Oral Culture, and Italian Americans,"* Palgrave-MacMillan, NYC, 2009.

As a concert artist, he has performed for audiences throughout the United States, Europe and South America including The Montreal Jazz Festival, Carnegie Hall, Alice Tully Hall at Lincoln Center, The Felt Forum, Guggenheim Museum, Metropolitan Museum of New York, Smithsonian Institute, Symphony Space, UCLA, the San Francisco World Music Festival, Central Park Summer Stage, the Jones Beach Theater, Eastern Europe, Italy, France, Germany, Belgium, Switzerland, Scotland and Brazil. In Brazil, he has returned several times to present concerts as a soloist and collaborator with Brazilian musicians produced by the Centro Cultural Banco do Brasil, Brasil Festeiro and SESC, in Sao Paulo and Porto Allegre.

His music appears on several labels including: Shanachie records, Meadowlark, Rounder Records, Lyrichord Disks, Ellipsis Arts, and Bribie records.

He has produced several recordings for his musical group I Giullari di Piazza of which he is the co-founder and musical director of the company in New York City. He appears as a musician playing in feature films including *When in Rome* (Touchstone films), *The Bounty Hunter* (Sony-Columbia) and Warner TV's *The Gossip Girls*.

He teaches at the Bergen Community College in Paramus, New Jersey and has taught at The Julius Hartt School of Music (University of Hartford); The Guitar Study Center of the New School in New York City; Sessione Sienese in Siena, Italy; SASI in Bratislava, Slovakia; and SESC in Sao Paulo, Brazil.

He is an artist in residence since 1994 at the Caramoor Center for Music and the Arts in Katonah, New York with the educational program on Italian renaissance music. He is also a composer for their "What's in a House" series for young students.

He holds a B.M. in Classical Guitar from the Hartt School of Music, Univ.of Hartford, (Hartford, Conn), M.M. in Jazz Studies and Arranging at William Paterson University (Wayne, N.J.); graduate studies in Ethnomusicology with Dr. Rose Brandel, at Hunter College of the City of New York, (NYC); Villa Schifanoia (Rosary College), in Florence, Italy: and the film music seminar with film composer, Ennio Morricone at the Accademia Chigiana in Siena, Italy.

Contact Information:

John T. La Barbera

Email: labmambo@aol.com
Website: www.myspace.com/johntlabarbera; www.johntlabarbera.com

The Songs

Desta l'amore, e nudre la Speranza IL BALLO con viva gioia una festiva danza.

Addio Mia Bella Addio

This romantic popular song is from the Risorgimento movement for the unification of Italy in 1848. It speaks about a lover going off to war and saying good-bye.

Strum Pattern: 4
Pick Pattern: 5

Alla Renella (A Tocchi A Tocchi)

This Roman song comes from the Risorimento (unification) period (1789-1870). It is a prisoner's love lament from the cells of in Rome's Reggina Celi prison. Alla Renella refers to Via de Trastevere, in Rome. The song is also known as "A tocchi, a tocchi."

*Strum Pattern:5
*Pick Pattern: 8

* *Tremolo sustained strumming use patterns at measure 17*

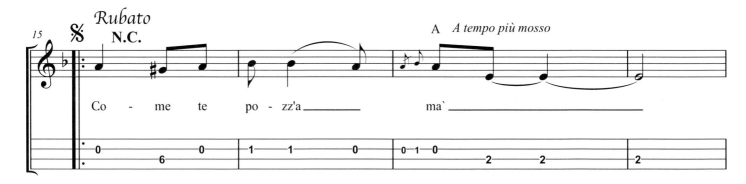

io me l'ho ri - so - late sta mma____ ti_____ na.
so' - ri - ma - sto solo a - bban - do - na_____

to. s'er pa - pa me do - na - sse tu - tta Ro - ma_____ e

me lo di - cesse la - ssa a - nnà chi t'a___ ma'_____ e

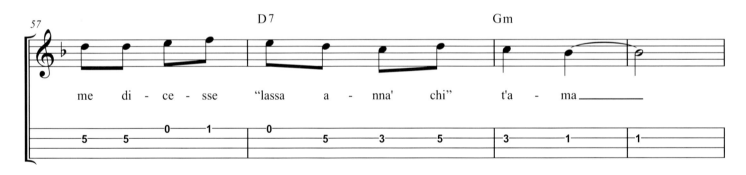

me di - ce - sse "lassa a - nna' chi" t'a - ma_____ e

io je di - re - bbe de "No, sa - gra co - ro - na."

24

Alla Renella piu` cresce er fiume
e piu` legna vie` a galla
piu` ve guardo e piu` ve fate bella.

A ttocchi a ttocchi la campana sona,
li turchi so' rivati alla marina.
Chi c'ha le scarpe rotte l'arisola,
io me l'ho risolate stammatina.

Come te pozz'ama`
come te pozz'ama`
S'esco da sti cancelli
quarchduno l'ha da paga`.

Amore, amore manneme un saluto
che sto a Reggina Celi carcerato,
d'amici e da parenti abbandonato
e so'rimasto solo abbandonato.

Come te pozz'ama....

S'er papa me donasse tutta Roma
e mi dicesse, "Lassa anna` chi t'ama"
e me dicesse "Lassa anna` chi t'ama"
io je direbbe, "No, sagra corona".

Come te pozz'ama....

The bells are ringing, and the Turks are coming.
If you have broken shoes, resole them
I resoled mine this morning.

How can I love you, if I escape from this prison,
someone will pay for it

My love send me a kiss. I am here abandoned
in Reggina Celi prison, and I remain alone and abandoned.

Amor Dammi Quel Fazzoletino

This is a very popular song from the Piemontese region, but also known all over Italy. It is a popular "ballo liscio" (ballroom dance).

Strum Pattern: 8, 9
Pick Pattern: 3, 4

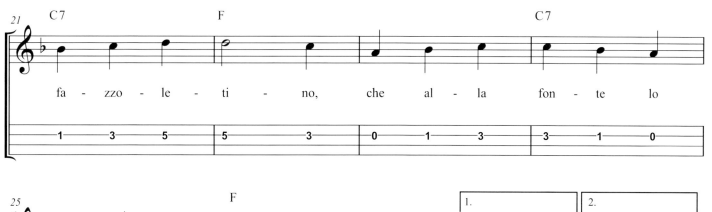

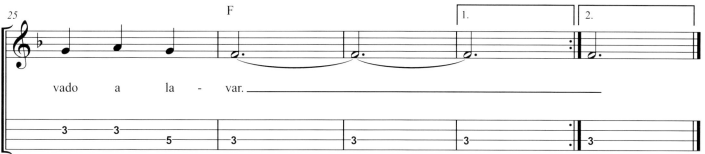

Amor dammi quel fazzolettino	Love give me that handkerchief
Amor dammi quel fazzolettino	Love give me that handkerchief
Che alla fonte lo vado a lavar.	I'm going to wash it at the fountain.
Te lo lavo con l'acqua e sapone	I'll wash it for you with soap and water
te lo lavo con l'acqua e sapone	I 'll wash it for you with soap and water
per ogni battuta un sospiro d'amor.	for each beat a sigh of love.
Te lo stendo su un ramo i rose	I'll place it down on a branch of the roses
il vento d'amore lo viene asciugar.	The winds of love will dry it.
Te lo stiro col ferro a vapore	I will press it with a steam iron
te lo stiro col ferro a vapore	I will press it with a steam iron
ogni pieghina è un bacino d'amor.	every fold is a reservoir of love.
Te lo porto di sabato sera	I'll bring it on Saturday night
te lo porto di sabato sera	I'll bring it to you a Saturday night
di nascosto di mamma e papà.	And I will hide it from Mom and Dad.
C'è chi dice l'amor non è bello	Some say love is not beautiful
c'è chi dice l'amor non è bello	some say love is not beautiful
certo quello l'amor non sa far.	of course, for those that don't know how.

Amore Mio Non Piangere (La Mondina)

This is a work song traditionaly sung by the women, called "mondina", who harvest the rice from the Po River Valley in Northern Italy. In this song, the young woman bids farewell to her loved one as she retuns home after leaving the rice fields.

Strum Pattern: 8, 9
Pick Pattern: 3, 4

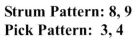

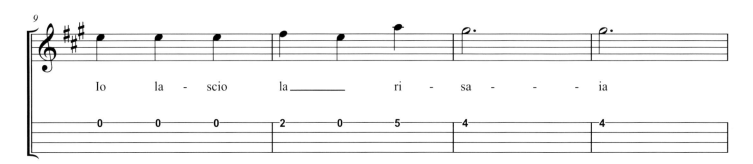

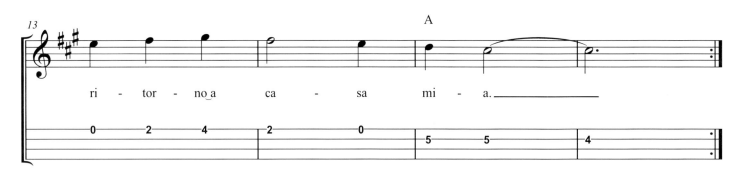

Amore mio no piangere
se me ne vado via
io lascio la risaia
ritorna a casa mia.

Vedo laggiu` tra gli alberi
La bianca mia casetta,
Vedo laggiu` sull' uscio
La Mamma che mi aspetta.

Mamma, papa' non piangere
Non sono piu` mondina,
Son ritornata a casa
A far la signorina

Mamma. papa' non piangere
Se sono consumata,
'E stata la risaia
Che mi ha rovinata.

'E stata la risaia
Che mi ha rovinata.
'E stata la risaia
Che mi ha rovinata.

Don't cry my love
 If I go away
I am leaving the rice fields
I am going back home.

I can see down below between the trees
my white house
I can see down there the doorway
where my mother is waiting for me.

Mommy, daddy, don't cry
I am no longer a young girl
I left the rice field
to become a young lady.

Mommy, daddy, don't cry
if I look consumed.
It was the rice fields
that ruined me.

It was the rice fields
that ruined me
It was the rice fields
that ruined me.

Ballo Tondo

The ballo tondo or ballo sardo is an anciient Sardinian round dance. It's origin are pre - Christian and Homer, the Greek poet, mentions the dance in Ulysses.

Strum Pattern: 10, 11
Pick Pattern: 4

Bella Bimba-Varda Che Passa La Villanella

This song is found throughout the Trentino Region of Northern Italy. It is a popular song with the Alpine and mountain choirs. The term "Villanella" refers to a beautiful young girl from the countryside dancing.

Strum Pattern:9
Pick pattern: 4

Canto di Cagliari

This folk song known as a "Canzoni" is from Cagliari, on the island of Sardinia. It speaks abouta beautiful garden and asks the gardener how much does it costs to buy a flower.

Strum Pattern: 5
Pick Pattern: 6

Andante ♩ = 100

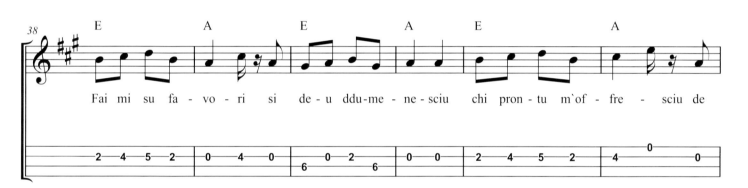

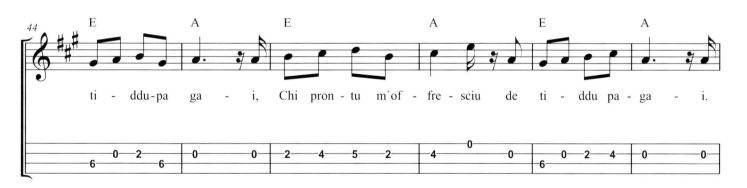

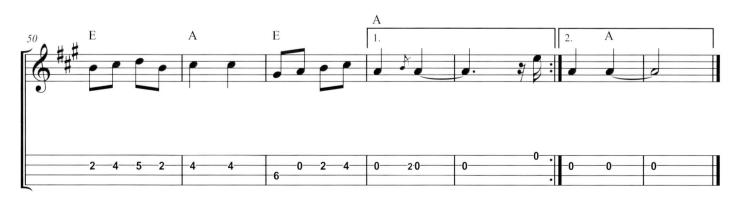

Canto di Cagliari
Guitar

Cecilia

This is one of the most popular narrative ballads found in all of the regions of Italy. This melody is from Pellestrina, Venice (Veneto). It is a story of a decieved woman who loses her honor in order to save her husband from prison and from death. After she consults her husband, already in prison, she submits to the captain only to find out that at dawn he was executed. This story was portrayed by composer Giacomo Puccini, in his opera Tosca.

Strum Pattern: 13, 14
Pick Pattern: 9, 10

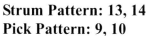

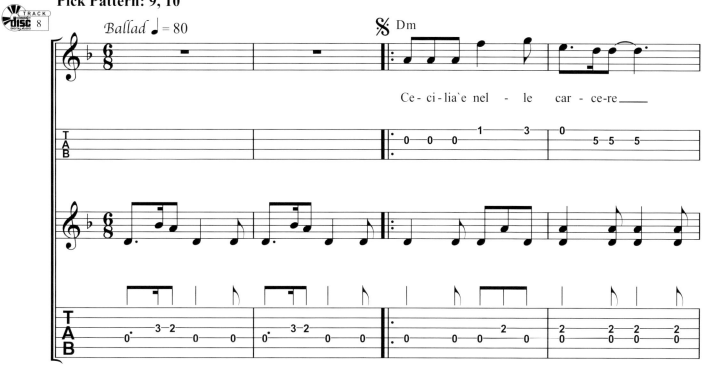

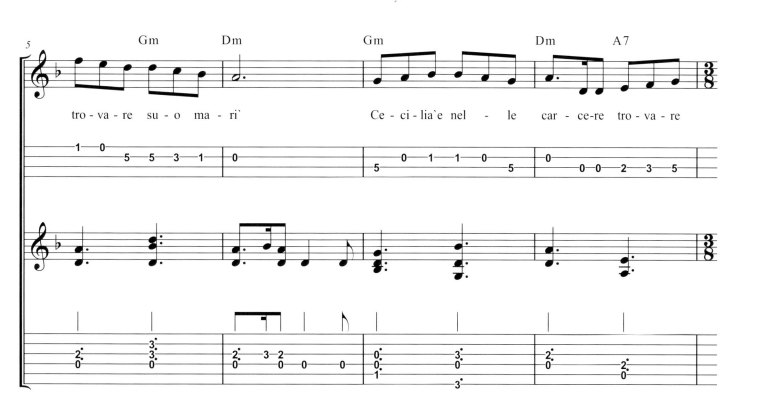

Cecilia 'e nelle carcere trovare suo mari
Cecilia 'e nelle carcere trovare suo mari
Caro marito mio na cosa t''o da di

Ghe 's 'e un capitano che 'l vol dormir con mi
Dormi dormi Cecilia salvi la vita a mi
Prepara i linsoi bianchi e 'l letto ben forni'

Cos''é la mezzanotte Cicilia da un sospir
Cara Cecilia cara che ti sospir cosi
Mi sento una 'smania al petto mi pare di morir

Cos''é la mezzanotte Cecilia va al balcon
la vede suo marito tacato a picolon
Bogia d'un capitano ti m''a tradio cosi

Ti me g'á tolto l'onore la vita al mio mari.

Cecilia is in prison to find her husband
Cecilia is in prison to find her husband
My dear husband there is something I have to tell you

There is a captain who wants to sleep with me
Sleep, sleep, my dear Cecilia, save the life of me
Prepare the white sheets and the neat bed

At the stroke of midnight, Cecilia sighs
My dear Cecilia, why do you sigh like so
I feel a 'frenzy in my chest that make me feel like I am dying

At the stroke of midnight Cecilia is on the balcony
There she sees her husband at the gallows hanged
Captain executioner, you have betrayed me such

You have already taken my honor and now my husband's life.

(The text to each verse have the same structure as the first one, except for the last two)

Cicerenella

One of the most popular Neapolitan tarantella from the 17th century. The ambiguous lyrics refer to Cicerenella, which means small chickpea. It is also known as a popular street song sung with improvisations on the text.

Strum Pattern: 16
Pick Pattern: 11

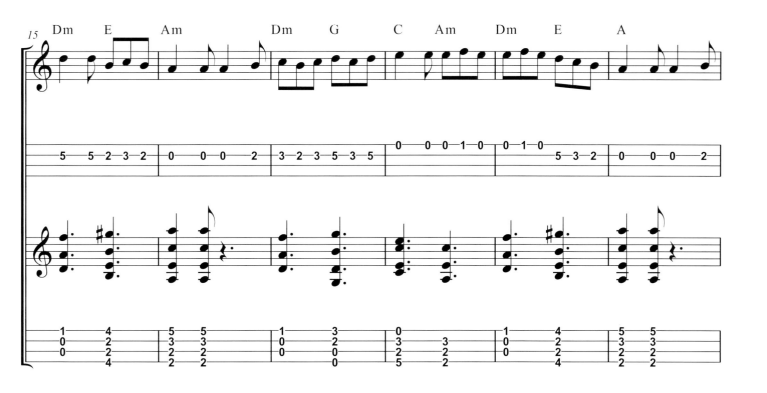

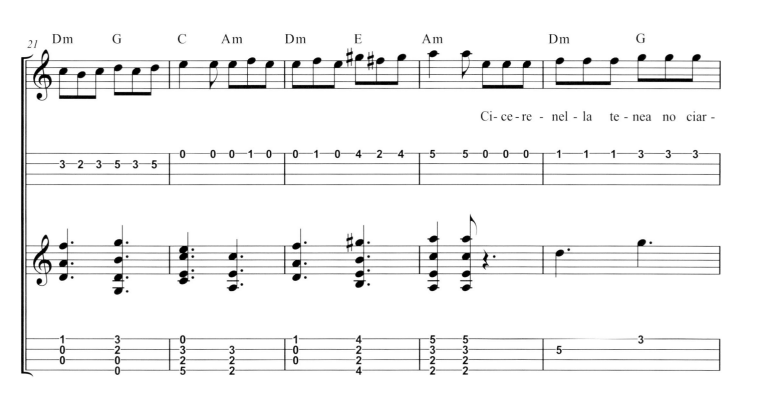

Ci - ce - re - nel - la te - nea no ciar -

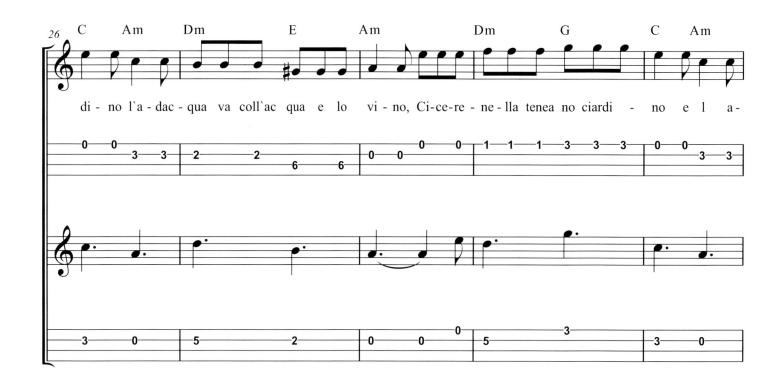

di - no l`a-dac-qua va coll`ac qua e lo vi - no, Ci-ce-re - ne - lla tenea no ciardi - no e l a-

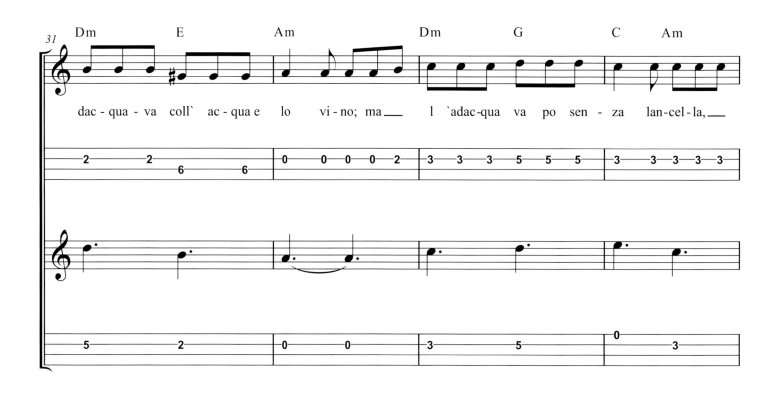

dac-qua - va coll` ac-qua e lo vi-no; ma__ l `adac-qua va po sen - za lan-cel-la,__

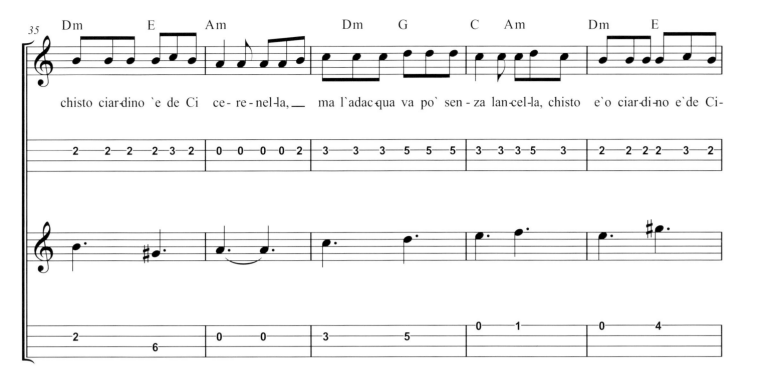

chisto ciar-dino `e de Ci ce - re - nel-la, ma l`adac-qua va po` sen - za lan-cel-la, chisto e`o ciar-di-no e`de Ci-

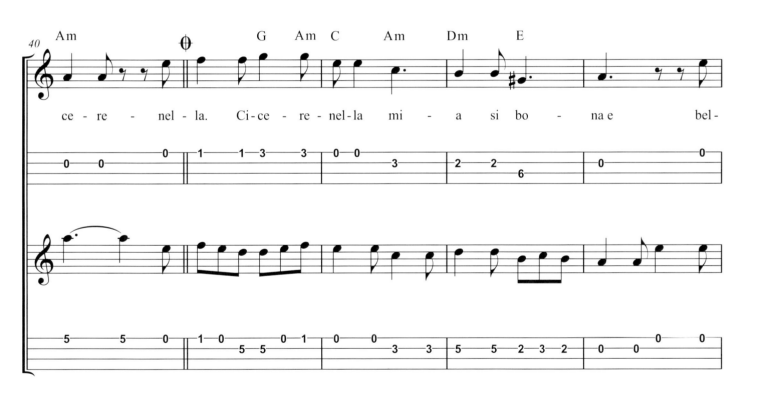

ce - re - nel - la. Ci-ce - re - nel-la mi - a si bo - na e bel-

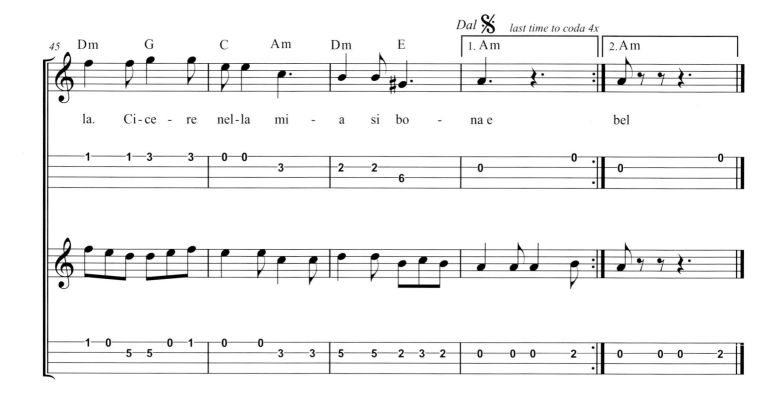

Cicerenella teneva no ciardino,
E l`acquava coll`acqua e lo vino.
Ma l`adacquava po senza lancella
Chisto ciardino `e Cicerenella
Cicerenella mia si bona e bella. (2x)

Cicerenella teneva no gallo,
Tutta la notte nce jeva a ccavallo,
Essa nce jeva po` senza la sella....
Chisto `e lo gallo de Cicerenella.
Cicerenella mia si bona e bella. (2x)

Cicerenella teneva no ciuccio
E ll`avea fatto no bello cappuccio,
Ma no tteneva ne ossa ne` pella...
Chisto `e lo ciuccio de Cicerenella.
Cicerenella mia si bona e bella. (2x)

Cicerenella had a garden
And she watered it with water and wine.
But she took care of it without a shovel,
This is the garden of Cicerenella
My Cicerenella is good and beautiful.

Cicerenella had a rooster,
All night long it would ride the horse,
But would ride it without a saddle,
This is the rooster of Cicerenella
My Cicerenella is good and beautiful.

Cicerenella had a mule,
And it had a beautiful hat,
But had no skin or bones,
This is the mule of Cicerenella.
My Cicerenella is good and beautiful.

Curenta della Val Chisone

A lively couple dance of the Val D'Aosta Region in Northern Italy.

Strum Pattern: 6
Pick Pattern: 7

Danza Corale Ciclica Carnevalesca

An ancient cyclical choral dance from Sicily, giving praise to Baccus, God of Wine.

Strum Pattern: 13, 14
Pick Pattern: 9, 10

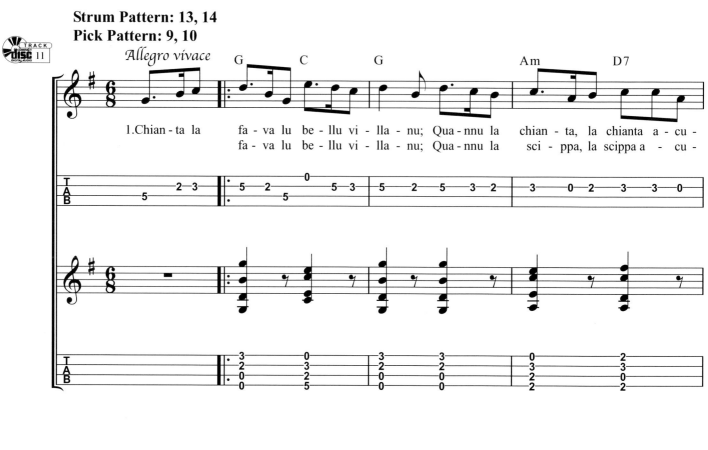

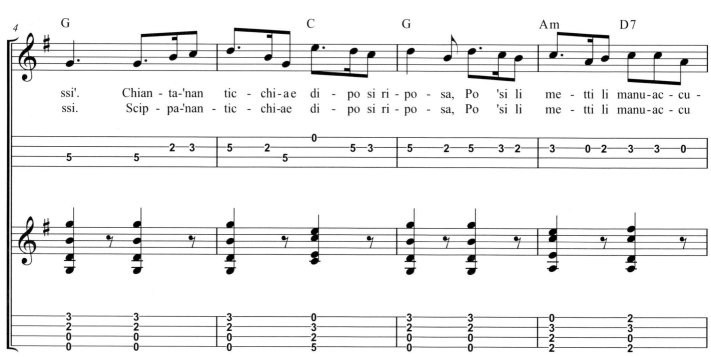

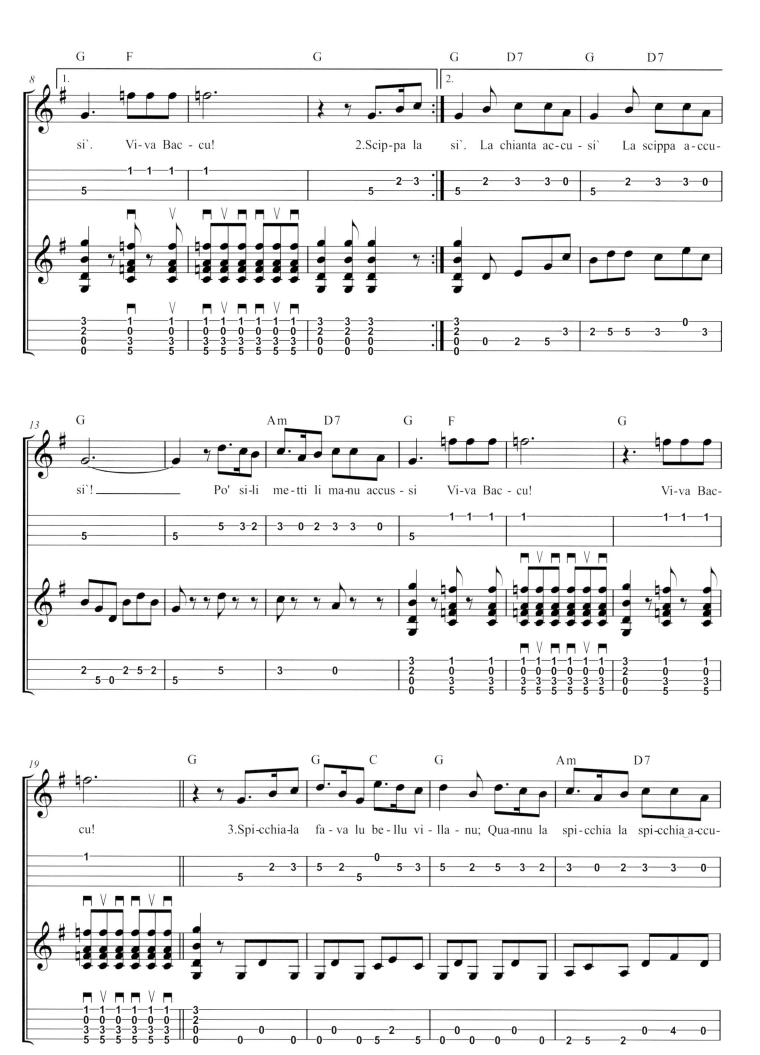

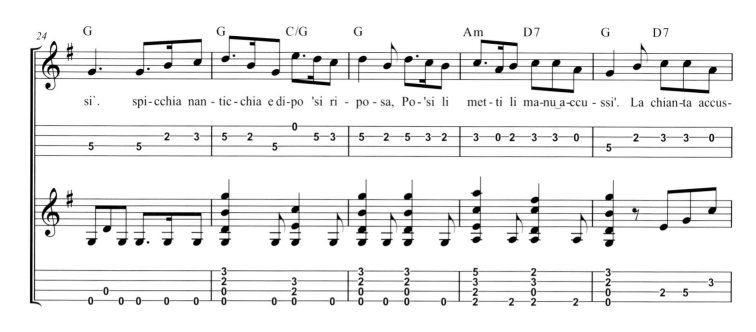

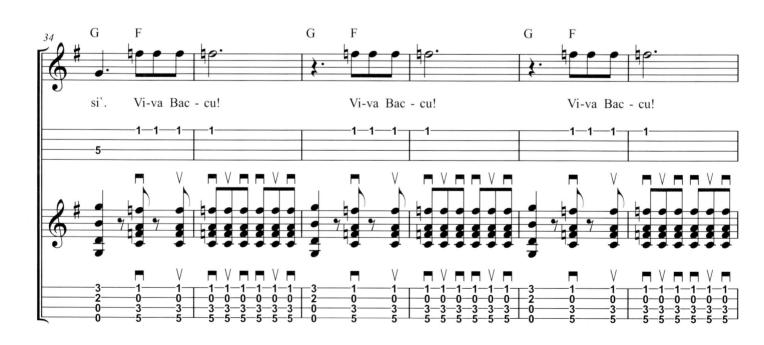

4.Co - ci la fa - va lu be - llu vi - lla - nu; Qua - nnu la co - ci, la co - cia e cus - si`. Co - ci' nan-

tic chia e di - po 'si ri - po - sa, Po 'si li met - ti li ma nu ac cus - si'. La chianta a - ccus-

si`, La scip pa accus - si' La co - ci accus - si'_____ Po 'si li met - ti li ma nu accus-

49

met-ti li ma nu accus - si'. La chian ta accus - si`, La scip pa accus - si' La co-ci accus - si', La man-cia accus-

si'_____ Po 'si li met - ti li ma nu accus - si`. Vi-va Bac - cu! Vi-va Bac-

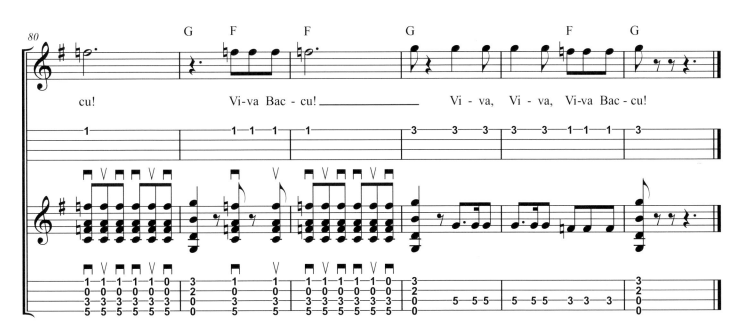

cu! Vi-va Bac-cu!_____ Vi - va, Vi - va, Vi-va Bac - cu!

1. Chianta la fava lu bellu villanu;
quannu la chianta, la chianta accusi'
Chianta 'nanticchia e dipo' si riposa,
Po' si li metti li manu accussi`.
    Viva Baccu!

The beautiful farmer plants the bean
When he plants it, he plants it like so
He plants a little, then he rests
Then he puts his hands like this;
    Hail to Baccus!

2. Scippa la fava lu bellu villanu;
Quannu la scippa, la scippa accussi`.
Scippa 'nanticchia e dipo'si riposa,
Po'si li metti li mani accussi'.
    La chiana accussi'
    La scippa accussi';
    Po'si li metti li manu accussi'.
    Viva Baccu!

The beautiful farmer tears the bean
When he tears it, he tears it like this
He tears it a little, then he rests
Then he puts his hands like this;
    He plants like this
    He tears like this;
    Then he puts his hands like this
    Hail to Baccus!

3. Spicchia la fava lu bellu villanu;
Quannu la spicchia, la spiccia accussi'.
Spicchia 'nanticchia e dipo' si riposa.
Po'si li metti li mani accussi'.
    La chianta accussi'
    La scippa accussi',
    La spicchia accussi';
    Po'si li metti li mani accussi'.
    Viva Baccu!

The beautiful farmer peels the bean
When he peels it, he peels it like this
He peels it a little, then he rests.
Then he puts his hands up like this.
    He plants it like this
    He tears it like this
    He peels it like this;
    Then he puts his hands like this.
    Hail to Baccus!

4. Coci la fava lu bellu villanu;
Quannu la coci, la coci accussi'.
Coci 'nanticchia e dipo'si riposa,
Po'si li metti li manu accussi'.
    La chianta accussi',
    La scippa accussi',
    La spicchia accussi',
    La coci accussi';
    Po'si li metti li manu accussi',
    Viva Baccu!

The beautiful farmer cooks the bean
When he cooks, he cooks it like this
He cooks it a little, then he rests.
Then he puts his hands up like this.
    He plants it like this
    He tears it like this
    He peels it like this
    He cooks it like this;
    Then he puts his hands like this.
    Hail to Baccus!

5. Mancia la fava lu bellu villanu;
Quannu la mancia, la mancia accussi'.
Mancia 'nanticchia e dipo'si riposa,
Po'si li metti li manu accussi'.
    La chianta accussi',
    La scippa accussi',
    La spicchia accussi',
    La coci accussi',
    La mancia accussi';
    Po'si li metti li manu accussi'.
    Viva Baccu!

The beautiful farmer eats the bean;
When he eats it, he eats it like this.
He eats it a little, then he rests.
Then he puts his hands up like this.
    He plants it like this
    He tears it like this
    He peels it like this
    He cooks it like this
    He eats it like this;
    Then he puts his hands up like this.
    Hail to Baccus!

Fateve 'Nnanze

This "ballo cantato" is a sung dance song from the Campagnia region. It's lyrics refer to dancing to the cetole, the colascione and the lute, all instruments from the 16th century that are related to the mandolin.

Strum pattern:16, 17
Pick Pattern: 11

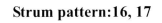
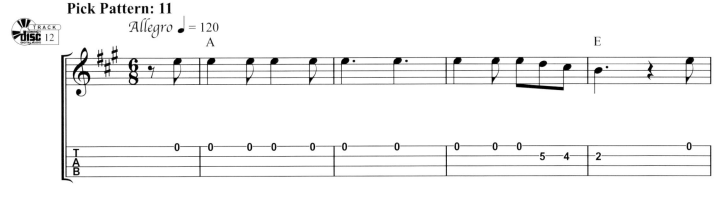

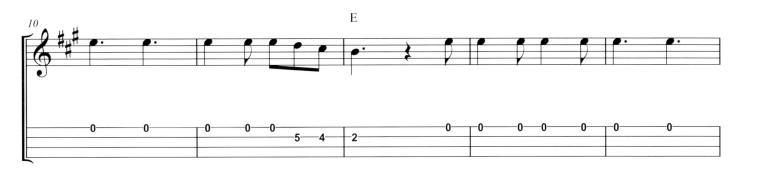
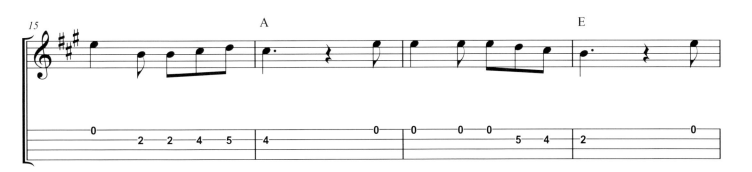

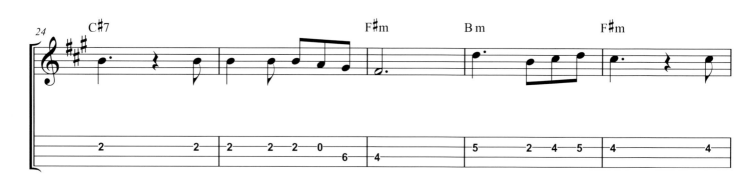

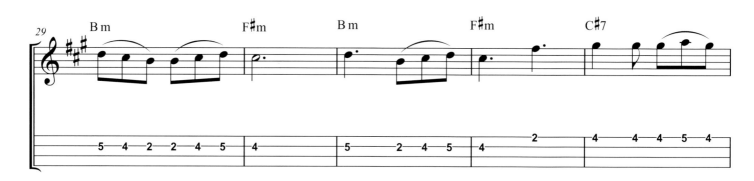

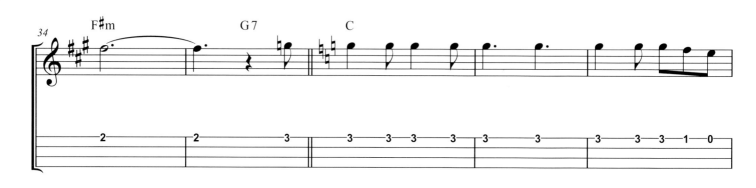

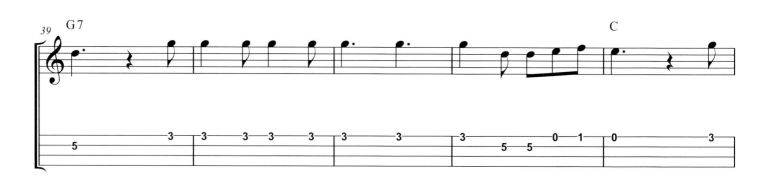

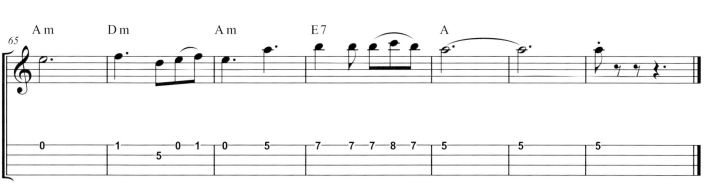

Fenesta Vascia

This is originally a "colascionata" from 16th century Naples. The colascione was a forrunner of the mandolin, and was also a popular instrument used in the commedia dell' arte. The music was later revised by Guglielmo Cottrau in 1825.

Strum Pattern: 13
Pick Pattern: 9, 12

Fenesta vascia, e patrona crudele,
quanta sospire m'aje fatto jettare!
M'arde sto core comm'a na cannella,
bella a quanno te sento annomenare!
Oje piglia la sperienza de la neve!
la neve `e fredda e se maniare,
e tu comme si` tant'aspra e crudele?
muorto mme vide e non mme vuo` ajutare?

Vorria arreventare no picciuotto
Co'na lancella a ghire vennenno acqua,
Pe mme nne i` da chiste palazzuotte:
Belle femmene meje, a chi vo` acqua?
Se vota na nennella da la'ncoppa
Chi `e sto ninno che va vennenno acqua?
E io responno co parole accorte:
So lagrime d'ammore, e non `e acqua!

Low Window, with a cruel mistress,
so many sighs you have bestowed on me!
This heart that burns like a candel
it is beautiful when I hear it!
Take the ungrateful snow for example!
The snow is cold and not affectionate,
and why are you so harsh and cruel?
Can't you see that I am dying, can't you help?

I 'd like to be a good boy
and go with a bucket to sell water
between these buildings and cry out:
"Oh my beautiful women, who wants to buy water?"
Then a young girl upstairs turns and says:
"Who is the handsome boy who sells water?"
then I would prudently answer her:
"They are tears of love, and not water."

Festa A Taormína

Traditional Sicilian festive tarantella from Taormina.

Strum Pattern: 17, 18
Picking Pattern: 11

I'Bambino `e della Mamma

This is a lullaby from Tuscany, near Florence. The translation means baby belongs to mommy and is sung to emphasize the strong relationship to an earthly family including: daddy, auntie, grandma as well as the divine, including the Madonna.

Strum Pattern: 4, 7
Pick Pattern: 7, 8

Lento

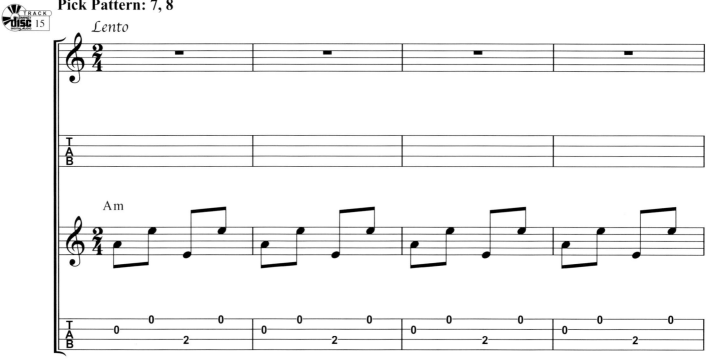

Ni - na   nan - na   nin - na   nan - na

1. Ninna nanna ninna nanna
i'bambino 'gli 'e della mamma
della mamma e della zia
della Virgine Maria.

2. Ninna nanna ninna nanna
i'bambino 'gli 'e della mamma
della mamma e della nonna
e di babbo quando torna.

3. Babbo babbo torna presto
i'bambino 'glt ha rotto i' testo
e l'ha rotto ni'canto di foco
babbo babbo pena poco.

4. Nanna-`o nanna-`o
i'bambino a chi lo do'?
e lo do' all'omo
che lo tenga un anno intero.

5. E lo do' alla befana
che lo tenga una settimana
e lo do' all omino di bronzo che la sera lo
porto a zonzo
e lo do' all'omino d'ottone, che
ci paga la pigione.

1. Rock-a-bye and rock-a-bye
Baby belongs to mommy
to mommy and to auntie
and to the Virgin Mary.

2. Rock-bye and rock-a-bye
baby belongs to mommy
to mommy and to grandma
and to daddy when he returns.

3. Daddy, daddy please come quick
baby has broken the pot's lid
he broke it near the hearth
Daddy, daddy come quickly.

4. Rock-a-bye and rock-a-bye
Who will I give this baby to?
I'll give him to the black man
that he might keep him an entire year.

5. And I'll give him to the good
Christmas witch that she might keep him a week.
And I'll give him to the bronze man
who will take him bye-bye in the evening
and I'll give him to the brass man
that he might pay his rent.

La Fiera De Mast'Andrea

This famous tarantella from 1845 is reflective of the popular music that influenced Opera Buffa, or Comic Opera in the true Neapolitan style. It is a real classic.

Strum Pattern: 15, 17
Pick Pattern: 11

67

li - no, nding-ghe-te ndin-ghe-te u cam - pa - niel - lo, ttu-pe-te ttu-pe-te u ta-mmur-ri - el - lo,ohie, Me-ne-

chel - la, ohie Me - ne - chie'. A la fie-ra de Mast' - An - dre - a m'ac - cat-taie no ca-la-

scio - ne, nfrun-ghe-te, nfrun-ghe-te u ca-la scio-ne, nfun-ghe-te, ndin-ghe-te u cam-pa - niel - lo, ttup-pe-te,

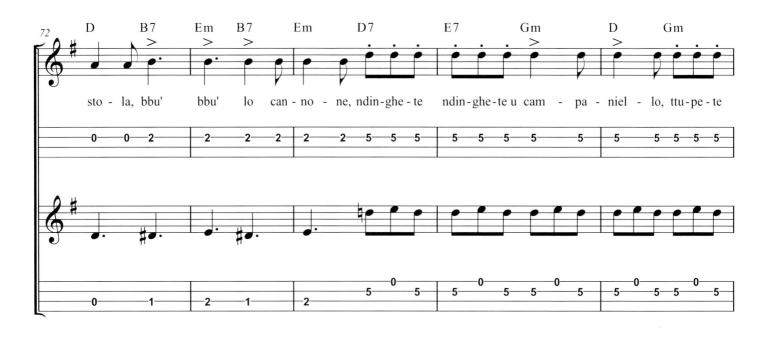

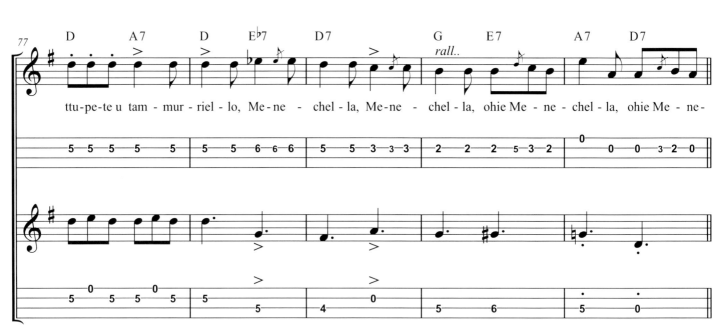

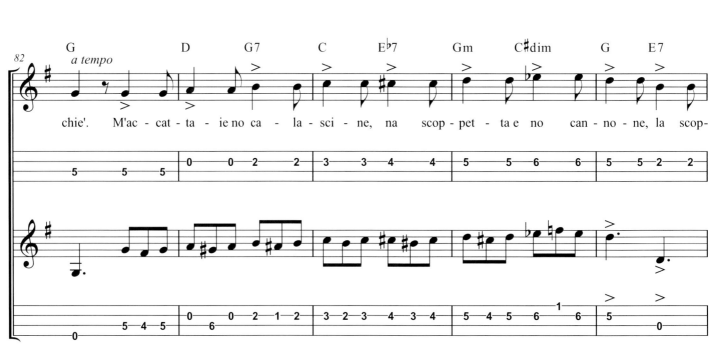

A la fiera de Mast` Andrea a m'accattaie campaniello,
ndinghete, ndinghete, u campaniello
ohie Menechella, ohie Meneche`!

A la fiera de Mast`Andrea a m`accattaie no tammurriello,
ttuppete, ttuppete il tammurriello,
ndinghete, ndinghete, u campaniello
ohie Menechella, ohie Menechiella,
ohie menechella, ohie Meneche`!

A la fiera de Mast'Andrea a m`accattaie no violino,
zichete zuchete u violino,
ndinghete, ndinghete, u campaniello,
ttuppete, ttuppete, u tammurriello
ohie Menechella, ohie Meneche`!

A la fiera de Mast'Andrea a m`accattaie no calascione,
nfrunghete, nfrunghete u calascione,
ndinghete, ndinghete u campaniello,
ttuppete, ttuppete u tammurriello,
zichete, zuchete u violino,
oihe Menechella, ohie Meneche`!

A la fiera de Mast'Andrea a me accattaie na scoppetta,
na pistola e nu canone, ppa` ppa` la scoppetta,
ppi`, ppi`, la pistola, bbu`, bbu` lo canone,
ndinghete, ndinghete u campaniello,
ttuppette, ttuppette u tammurriello,
Menechella, Menechella, ohie Menechella, ohie Meneche`!

M'accattaie no calascione, na scoppetta e no cannone,
la scoppetta ppa` ppa`, lo cannone bbu` bbu`,
ppa` ppa`, bbu`, ppa` ppa` ppa`, bbu`.

(At the feast of Mast'Andrea I bought a bell, a tambourine
a violin, a calascione, a broom, a pistol, and a canon.
Oh dear treasure of mine, I give them all to you!)

La Furlana

La Furlana is one of the many types of instrumental dances that came originally from the Venitian provence of Friuli. It was a favorite Venetian dance in the 17th century. Both the dance and the music vary in each village. This version of the dance is from Frassinoro, Modena, in the region of Emiglia.

Strum Pattern: 20, 21
Pick Pattern: 16

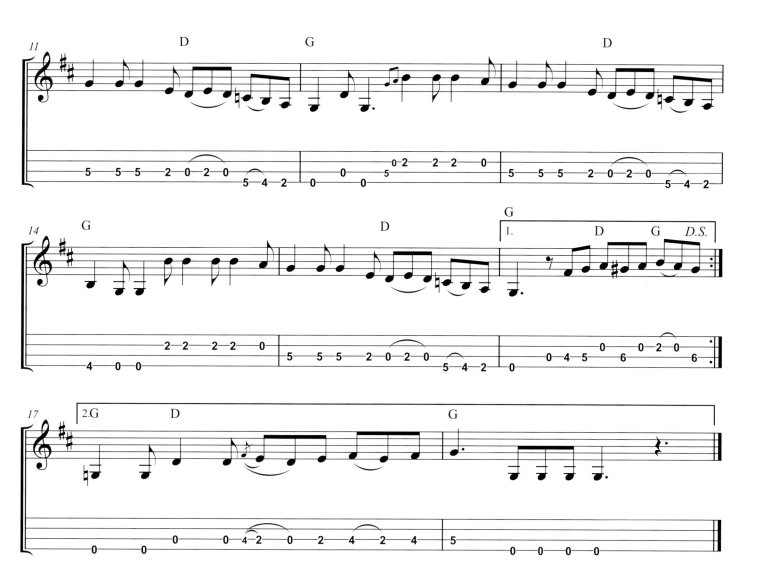

La Luna `Nta Sta Ruga

Pastoral saltarello from Calabria.

Strum Pattern: 17, 18
Pick Pattern: 12

La Manfredina

From the collection of 14th century Italian dances found in the British Museum's Library. La Manfredina also derives from the Manferrina from the northern Italian Piedmont district of Monferrat.

Strum Pattern: 4, 7
Pick Pattern: 7

Andante ♩ = 103

La Monferrina

La Monferrina, from the northern Italian region of Piemonte, is a traditional couple dance done within a circle that continues as other couples re-enter within the circle. It can be an instrumental dance as well as sung.

Strum Pattern: 4
Pick Pattern: 6

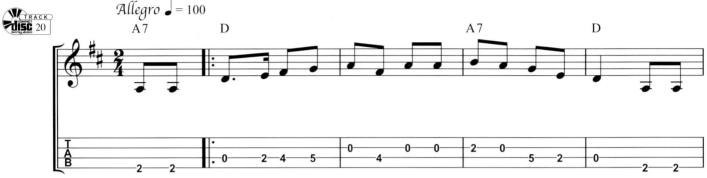

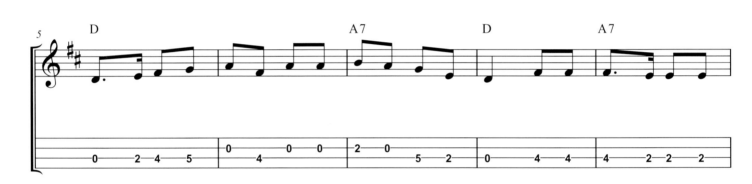

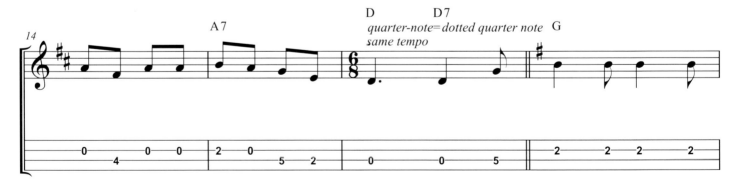

La Principessa di Carini

This is one of the best known narrative songs from Sicily, passed down through oral tradition by storytellers. It tells of the tragic "crime of honor" that happened in 1563. According to the text, the princess was murdered in the castle by her father, the Baron of Carini, for having an adultress love affair with the knight Ludovico Vernagallo, supposedly her cousin.

Strum Pattern: 20, 23
Pick Pattern: 16

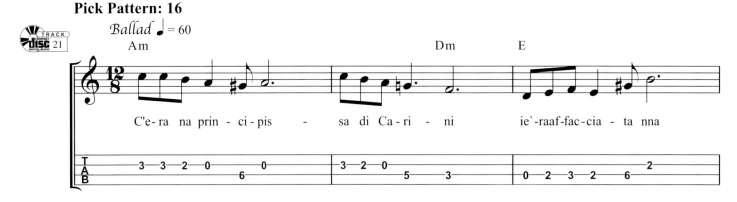

C'era 'na principissa di Carini,
iera affacinata nna lu so barcuni
Viri viniri'na cavalleria:
Chist' `e me patri chi beni pi mia.
O caru patri, chi beniti a fari?
O cara figghia, p'ammazzar'a tia.
O caru patr'un m'ammazzati ora,
quantu va chiamu a lu me confissuri.
'Nta tantu tempu 'un t' `ai confussatu,
ora ti vinni sta cunfissioni.
Tira, cumpagnu mia, nun la sgarrari!
pichila nna lu centru di lu cori!
Lu primu corpu la donna cariu;
secunnu corpu la donna muriu.
Curriti tutti monici e parrini
ora ch' `e morta la vostra signura!
Li vermi si la mancinu la `ula
unni c' `e misa la bedda `ulera.
E idda si scantava a dormiri sula
ora cu l'autri morti accumpagnata.

There was a Princess of Carini
she looked out from her balcony
She saw knights riding toward her:
This is my father who comes for me.
Oh dear father why have you come?
Oh dear daughter, to kill you
Oh father don't kill me now;
I want to call my confessor.
You haven't confessed in a long time
now take this confession.
Strike, my friend, don't miss!
Strike her in the center of the heart
At the first strike the woman falls;
at the second the woman dies.
Run, monks and priests,
now that your lady is dead!
Worms eat her throat,
there where the beautiful necklace lies,
She feared sleeping alone
now she sleeps with the dead.

La Quadrighia

The Sicilian version of the quadrille, a lively popular dance from the nineteenth century. It is similar to a square dance between four couples.

Strum Pattern: 13, 14
Pick Pattern: 9, 10, 11

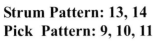

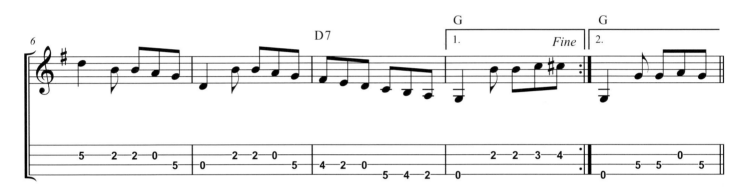

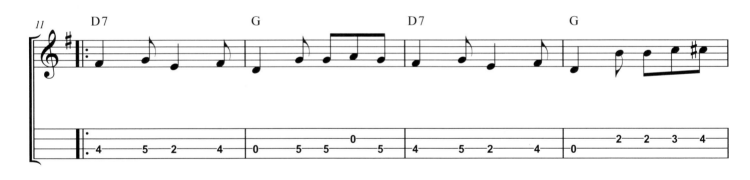

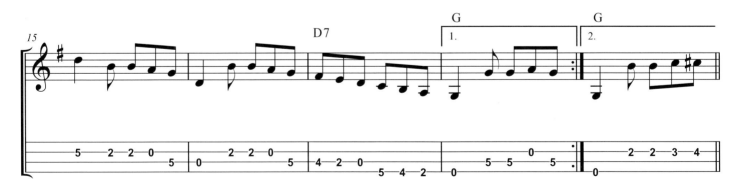

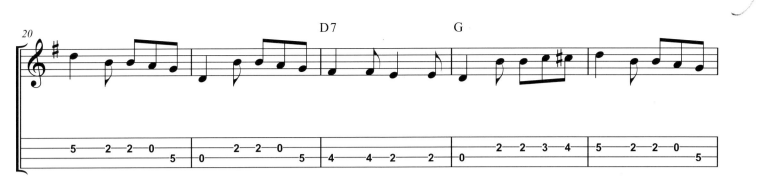

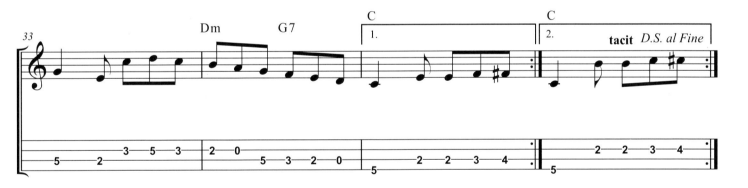

La Rotta

This anonymous piece is one of the best examples of Italian medieval dance music from a 14th century manuscript found in the British Library. It is also one of the few existing instrumental pieces from the Italian Trecento period.

Strum Pattern: 4, 7
Pick Pattern: 5, 7

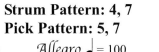

Allegro ♩ = 100

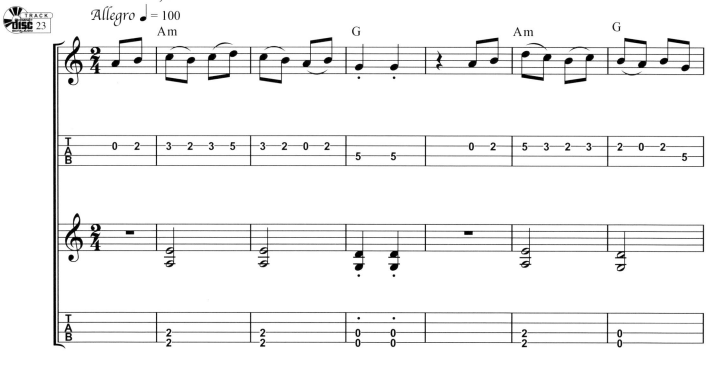

La Serpe A Carolina

This song is based on an eighteenth century aire. It is a parody criticizing the Bourbon Queen, Maria Carolina who reigned in Naples (1752-1814). It criticizes her for interfering in politics and for having many lovers.

Strum pattern: 12
Pick Pattern: 13, 14, 15

Ballad ♩ = 60

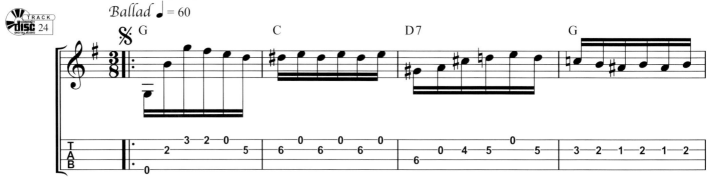

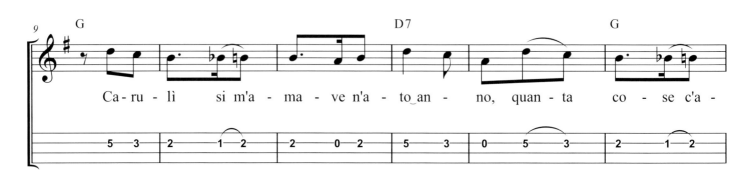

Ca - ru - lì si m'a - ma - ve n'a - to an - no, quan - ta co - se c'a -

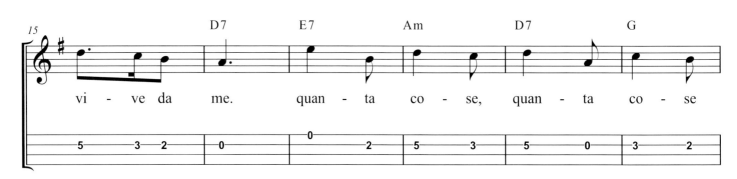

vi - ve da me. quan - ta co - se, quan - ta co - se

90

quan - ta co - se c'a vi - ve da me. ma sì paz - za e già

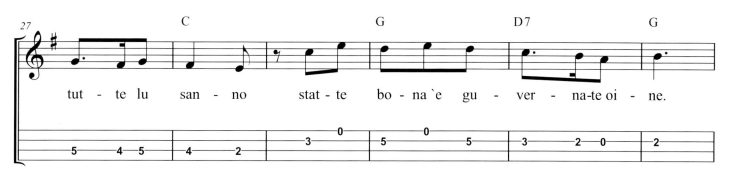

tut - te lu san - no stat - te bo - na `e gu - ver - na-te oi - ne.

ma si paz - za e già tut - te lu san - no

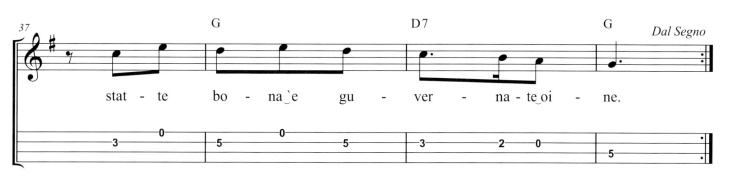

stat - te bo - na `e gu - ver - na - te oi - ne.

Dal Segno

Caruli si m'amave n'ato anno,
quanta cosa c'avive da me.
quanta cose, quanta cose
quanta cose c'avive da me.
Ma si pazza e gia` tutte lu sanno
statte bona e guvernate oine`. (2x)

`Nu vurzone de doppie de Spagna
lu tenevo io apposta pe'te,
ma scuperta s'`e gia la magagna
statte bona e guvernate oine'.

Carammanico cchiu` de sett'anne
cuffiato buono da te
ma si zoccola e tutte lu sanno
statte bona e guvernate oine`.

Cu l'arsenico tu lo sciusciate
munzu' Attuono accussi` cuntentaste
mo' ca saccio ca tutte lu sanno
statte bbona e guvernate oine'.

Carolina if you loved me another year
so many things you would have had from me.
but you are crazy and everyone knows it
So long, and take care of yourself.

A sack of Spanish loot
I saved for you
but now, everyone knows about it.
So long, and take care of yourself.

Carammanico , for more than seven years
was bewitched by you
you are a loose woman and everyone knows
So long and take care of yourself

With poison you killed him
so you kept Mr. Attuono happy for yourself
but now I know that everyone understands the crime
So long and take care of yourself.

La Veneziana

This type of dance from Modena, in Emiglia-Romagna, is common in all of Central Italy.

Strum Pattern: 21
Pick Pattern: 16

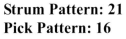

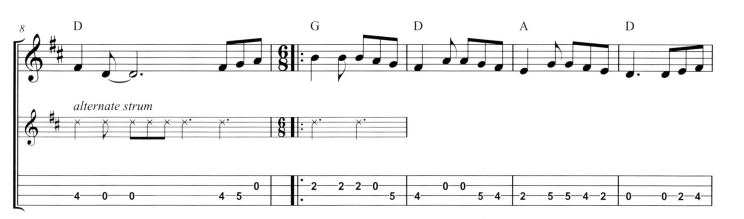

alternate strum

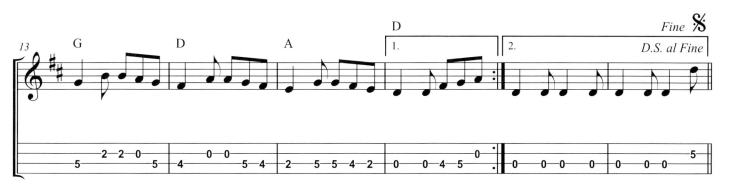

La Vo`

This lullaby from Sicily is filled with many magical images in the imagination of a child but also tells of the mother's hardships in childbirth.

Strum Pattern: 15, 19
Pick Pattern: 9, 11

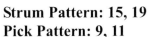

Adagio ♩ = 60

o, dor - mi be - dda, fai la vo`.

Vinniressi lu jornu e lu momentu
To matri quannu a latu ti ritrovo'
Dopu di novi misi cu'granni stentu
Mamma facist'` e `n frunde ti vasso`.

Dormi nicuzza cu `l`angili do'
Dom'e riposa, ti cando la vo`
O, o, o, dormi bedda, fai la vo`.

Si `nti lu cielu calassi `na fata
Non lu putissi fare ssu splinnuri
Ca sta facennu tu, birdizza amata
Da ssa nacuzza di rose e di sciuri.

Dormi nicuzza cu `l`angili do'
Dom'e riposa, ti cando la vo`
O, o, o, dormi bedda, fai la vo`

Came the day and the moment
when your mother found you by her side
After nine months, with great hardship
Mother made you and kissed your brow.

Sleep, little one, sleep with the angels
Sleep and rest, I sing you a lullaby
Oh, Oh, Oh, sleep my beauty, rock-a-bye.

If from the heavens a fairy descended
it could not match the splendor
That you are radiating, my adorned beauty,
In that little cradle of roses and flowers.

Sleep, little one, sleep with the angels
Sleep and rest, I sing you a lullaby,
Oh, Oh, Oh, sleep my beauty, rock-a-bye
Rock, rock, rock, sleep my beauty, rock-a-bye.

97

Michelemma`

This Neapolitan song dates back to the 1600's. Its translation has different meanings. One refers to the tale of a beautiful woman, Michela, who had been taken captive by Saracen pirates. It can also refer to the island of Ischia, off the coast of Naples, a place often invaded by Saracen pirates. The "scarola", or escarlole, can refer to a curly haired girl or the rocky landscape of the island. Michelemma` means Michela is mine. The song became popular among fishermen.

Strum Pattern: 13, 14
Pick Pattern: 9, 11

E nata miezzo mare
Michelemma` Michelemma`
E nata miezzo mare
Michelemma` Michelemma`
oje na scarola, oje ne scarola.

Li Turche se `nce vanno
Michelemma` Michelemma` 2x
a riposare, a riposare.

Viato a chi la vence
Michelemma`, Michelemma` 2x
co sta figliola, co sta figliola.

`E `mpieto porta na
Michelemma` Michelemma` 2x
Stella Diana, Stella Diana

Chi pe la cimma e chi
Michelemma` Michelemma`2x
pe lo streppone, pe lo streppone.

Sta figlola ch` 'e figlia
Michelemma` Michelemma` 2x
Oje de Notare, oje de Notare,

Pe fa mori` l'amante
Michelemma` Michelemma` 2x
a duje a duje, a duje a duje.

She was born in the middle of the sea
Michelemma` Michelemma`
She was born in the middle of the sea
Michelemma` Michelemma`
a curly haired woman, a curly haired woman.

The Turks go there
Michelemma` Michelemma`
to rest, to rest.

Bless the one who wins
Michelemma` Michelemma`
with this beautiful girl.

And on his chest he wears
Michelemma` Michelemma`
the Star of Diana.

Those on the top
Michelemma` Michelemma`
and those on the bottom.

This grl is the daughter
Michelemma` Michelemma`
of the Notary.

To kill the lovers
Michelemma` Michelemma`
two by two.

Pizzica Tarantata

This Pizzica is from the Salento region of Puglia. The pizzica is a fast frenetic dance played during the healing ritual of a "tarantata", the person being cured by this music. It emphasis the lydian mode, and the lyrics ask for the help of Saint Paul, the patron saint of the tarantati.

Strum Pattern: 22
Pick Pattern: 16

100

A-ddo' te piz - zi - ca - ta oi li' oi -

la'_____ A-ddo' te piz - zi - ca - ta oi - li   oi - la_____ so - tto allu gi - ru

gi-ru___ so-tto allu gi-ru   gi-ru___ so-tto allu gi-ru   gi-ru de la go-nne - lla.

Quel Mazzolin Di Fiori

> From the Piemonte region of Northern Italy. This is one of the most famous folk songs of the Alpini, the mountain infantry of the Italian Army, who are well known for their songs and choirs.

Strum Pattern: 1, 2
Pick Pattern: 2

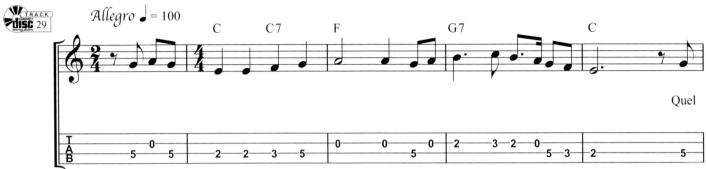

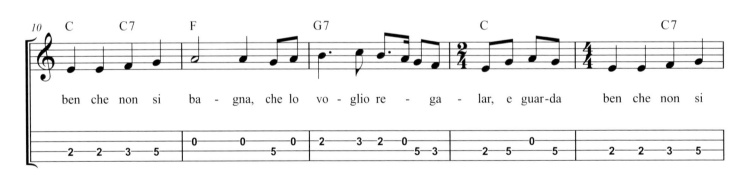

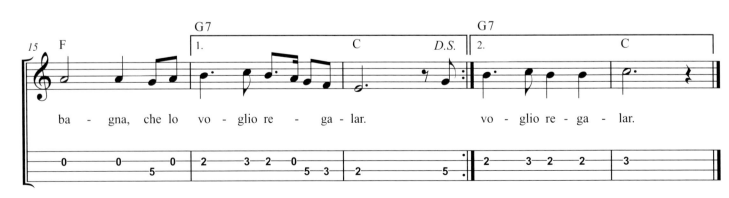

Quel mazzolin di fiori
Che vien della montagna, (twice)
E guarda ben che no 'l se bagna
Che lo voglio regalar. (twice)

Lo voglio regalare
Perchè l'è un bel mazzetto. (twice)
Lo voglio dare al mio moretto
Questa sera quando 'l vien. (twice)

Sta sera quando 'l viene
Gli fo'na brutta cera (twice)
E perchè sabato di sera
Ei no l'è vegnù da me. (twice)

No l'è vegnù da me,
L'è andà dalla Rosina. (twice)
E perchè mi son poverina,
Mi fa pianger e sospirar. (twice)

Mi fa pianger e sospirare
Sul letto dei lamenti. (twice)
E che mai dirà la gente ?
Cosa mai diran di me? (twice)

Diran ch'io son tradita,
Tradita nell'amore (twice)
E a me mi piange il cuore,
E per sempre piangerà. (twice)

Abbandono il primo,
Abbandono il secondo, (twice)
Abbandono tutte il mondo
E non mi marido più. (twice)

This bunch of flowers
That comes from the mountains (twice)
Take care not to get it wet
Because I want to give it as a gift. (twice)

I want to give it away
Because it is a beautiful small bouquet. (twice)
I want to give it to my dark-haired man
Tonight when he comes. (twice)

Tonight when he comes
I'll look like a sorry sight to him
Because Saturday evening
He doesn't come to me. (twice)

He didn't come to me
He went to Rosina's house . (twice)
And because I am so sad.
He makes me weep and sigh. (twice)

He makes me weep and sigh
on a bed of tears. (twice)
and what else will people say?
What will they say about me? (twice)

They will say I'm betrayed
Betrayed in love. (twice)
And my heart cries out
And will always cry. (twice)

The first one abandoned me
the second one abandoned me, (twice)
everyone abandoned me
And I will never marry . (twice)

Re Gilardin

This is one of the most famous narrative ballads from Alessandria, in the Piedmont region of northern Italy. Both poetic and tragic, a young king is killed in battle while his wife is recovering from childbirth. At the church, she realized that she is at his funeral as he finally appears as a ghost and tells her that he has returned to earth.

Strum Pattern: 12
Pick Pattern: 13

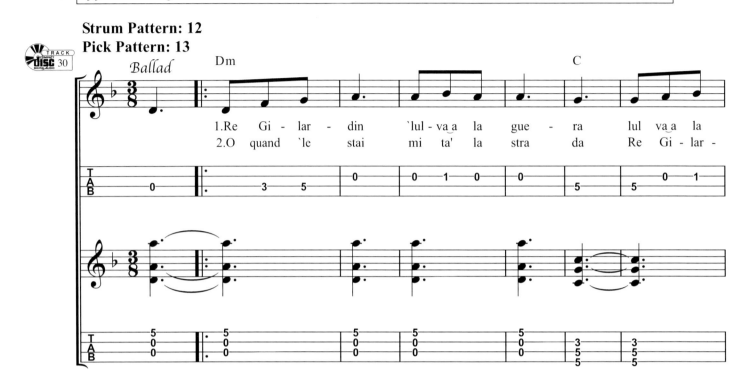

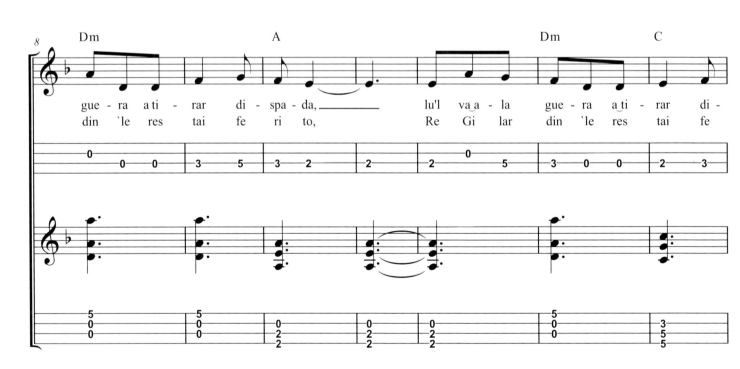

Re Gilardin lu `l va a la guerra
lu `l va a la guerra a tirar a spada
lu 'l va a la guerra a tirar a spada

O quand `l 'e stai mita` la spada
Re Gilardin `l 'e restai ferito. 2x

Re Gilardin ritorna `ndietro
dalla sua mamma vo `nda' morire. 2x

O tun, tun, pica a la porta
o mamma mia, che mi son morto. 2x

O pica pian caro `l mio figlio
che' la to dona `l g`a' `n picul fante. 2x

Ca sia `n fil ca `l sia una fiola
che sensa padre deve restare. 2x

O si e' `n fio mandel'a scola
si l`e' un fila mandela monica. 2x

O madona, la mia madona
cosa vuol dire ch`i sonan tanto? 2x

O nuretta, la mia nuretta
j g'fan 'legria al tuo fante. 2x

O madona, la mia madona
disem che giorno `o da alsarmi? 2x

Alsati anco', alsati domani
`alsati 'n po' quando ti pare. 2x

O madona, mia madona
disem che moda o' da vestirmi? 2x

Vestati di rosso, vestati di nero
ma le brunette stanno piu` bene. 2x

O quand l`e stai 'nt l'us de la chiesa
d'un girighello si l`a incontrato:
bundi', bungiur an voi, vedovella. 2x

O, no, no no, che non so vedovella
g'o `l fante 'n cuna e `l marito in guerra.2x

O si', si', si', che vui sei vedovella
vostro mari' l`e trei di` che 'l fa terra. 2x

O tera o tera aprati `n quatro
voglio vedere il mio cuor reale. 2x

La tua boca la sa di rose
`nvece la mia la sa di terra. 2x.

King Gilardin he goes to war
He goes to war to wield his sword
He goes to war to wield his sword.

Oh when he reached mid-road
King Gilardin was wounded. 2x

King Gilardin turns back
Back to his mother he wants to die. 2x

Oh tap, tap, tap, he knocks on the door
oh my mother, I am dying. 2x

Oh knock softly my dear son
because your wife has had a babe. 2x

Be it a son, or be it a daughter
it will be without a father. 2x

Oh if it is a son send him to school
if it is a daughter make her a nun. 2x

Oh my lady, my lady
why do they ring the bells so? 2x

Oh dear daughter-in-law, my dear daughter-in-law
They are celebrating your dear child's birth. 2x

Oh lady, my lady
on which day shall i rise? 2x

Rise today, rise tomorrow
rise when you please. 2x

Oh lady, my lady
tell me how shall I dress? 2x

Dress in red, dress in black
but dark shades are best. 2x

Oh when she was at the entrance of the church
An altar boy met her
Good day, good morning to you young widow.

Oh, no,no,no, I am not a widow
I have a new born in the cradle and a husband at war. 2x

Oh, yes, yes, yes, you are a widow!
It is three days that your husband turns to earth. 2x

Oh earth, oh earth, open in fours!
I want to see my royal heart. 2x

Your mouth tastes of roses
while mine tastes of earth. 2x

Rumanele

This is a strambotto from Cento,(Ferrara) in the province of Emiglia. The strambotto is one of the oldest Italian verse forms dating back to the renaissance. It is composed of a single stanza of an eleven sylable line. The subject was generally about love, as in this piece.

Strum Pattern: 8, 9
Pick Pattern: 3, 4

la - dri si chi-man gio-vi no-ti i-na-mo-ra_____ ti._____ In sa.

Guarda che bel seren se non se nuvola
che bela note de rubar le done
chi ruba done non si chiaman ladri
si chiaman giovinoti inamorati

In mez al mer a gh`e` un alberiein
c'tot i ann al prudus da gia` fiurein
toti el `zouvni el garden al colore
e quisti i en i fiurein de l'amore

S'as fus na rundanena per un'ora
vuria vuler indov al mio bein lavora
gli vuria der un bagio in dla buchena
vuria bein dir c'e` sta` la rundanena

L`e' pur al bel serein se non s'anuvla
o pur un bel murous se non mi burla
l' pur al bel serein se non si guasta
o pur un bel morous se non mi lasia.

Look what a peaceful evening, if the clouds don't come.
Oh what a beautiful night to steal a woman's heart.
Who steals her heart should not be called a thief.
They should be called a young lover.

In the midst of the sea, there is a small tree that
produces beautiful flowers. All young people
look at their color, these are the
flowers of love.

If I were a swallow for just one hour
I'd like to go where my loved one works
I would give a kiss on the mouth, then I would say
the swallow did it.

It's a very peaceful evening if the clouds don't come
or a beautiful lover, if I don't sound funny, it is a
peaceful night if it doesn't rain, or a beautiful lover,
if she (he) dosn't leave me.

Schiarazula Mirazula

Popular renaissance folk dance from the Pierre Phalese dance book, published in 1583. Attributed to Georgio Mainerio 1535-1582.

Strum Pattern: 6
Pick Pattern: 5, 7

Si Li Femmene Purtassero la Spada

Anonymous 16th Century Neapolitan Villanella . "If women carried swords, sad would be the man who loves her for he would be tormented not only by her beauty, but by the sword."

Strum Pattern: 4
Pick Pattern: 7

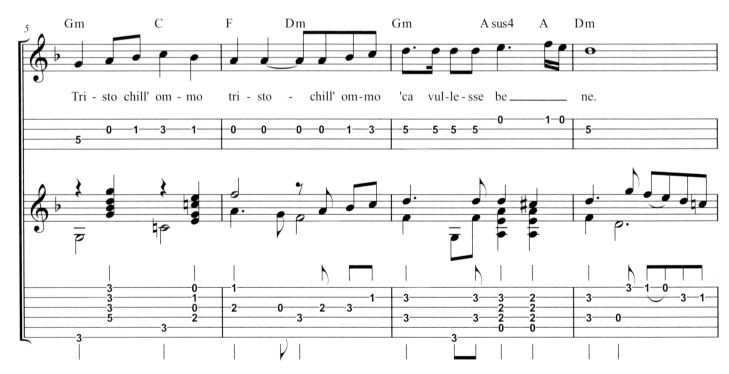

113

Si li Femmene, si li femmene purtassero la spada.
tristo chill'ommo ca vulesse bene
a donna ca lu cor crudele tene.

Pecche' nun solo lu turmentaria
colli belizze ma co' la spada ancora
mille ferite le darria ogn'hora.

E ne saccio una ch 'e tanto crudele
ca si uno la guardasse dicarria;
pecche' me guardi? E po l'accidarria.

Forse 'e buono ca nun portano ll'arme
ma chianellette e trezze e verducate
pe' ffa' murire mille 'nnammurate.

114

Tarantella alla Montemarinese

Traditioal tarantella from Montemarano, in Campania, performed for the Carneval celebrations before Lent. This tarantella is based on a theme with variations which are usually improvised. The syncopated rhythmic accompaniment is a particular trait of the tarantellas from this town.

Variation 1

Variation 2

Tarantella Calabrese

A very lively tarantella in the Calabrese style.

Strum Pattern: 18, 17, 19 with 15
Pick Pattern: 11

Tarantella Spiritusa

This is a very lively and spirited tarantella from Sicily.

Strum Pattern: 17, 18
Pick Pattern: 11, 12

Track 6

119

Riciulina. Metzetin

Tutti Mi Dicon Maremma Maremma

The Maremma is in the southwest corner of Tuscany, once an uninhabitable marshland plagued by malaria and bandits until the early nineteenth century. This Tuscan song is a lament about the bitter sorrow of the loved ones who have left and failed to return.

Strum Pattern: 9
Pick Pattern: 3

Adagio ♩ = 60

Tutti mi dicon Maremma Maremma
e a me mi pare una Maremma amara
l'uccello che ci va perde le penne
Io ci `o perduto una persona cara.

Sia maledetta Maremma Maremma
sia maledetta Maremma e chi l'ama
sempre mi trema il cuor quando ci vai
perche' ho paura che non torni mai

They all tell me Maremma, Maremma
but for me it seems like a bitter Maremma
birds that go there lose their feathers
and I lost my very dear love there.

Cursed be the Maremma Maremma
cursed be the Maremma and those who love it
my heart always trembles when you go
because I fear that you will never return.

Vieni Sul Mar

This traditional song became a popular classic with many famous Italian Opera singers including Enrico Caruso in the early Twentieth century.

Strum Pattern: 8, 9
Pick Pattern: 3, 4

Tempo di Waltz ♩ = 145

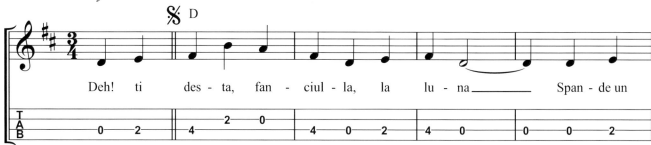

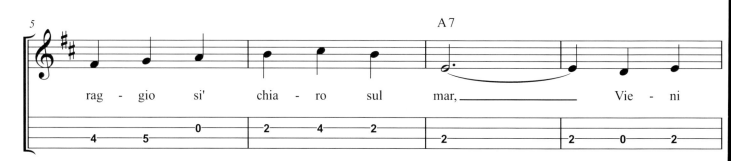

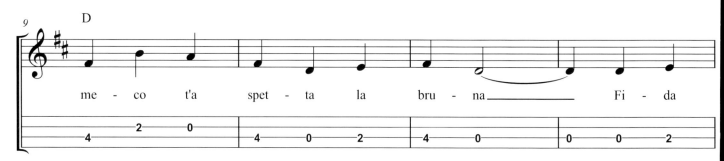

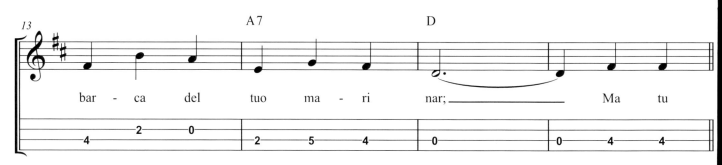

Deh! ti desta, fanciulla, la luna
Spande un raggio si' chiaro sul mar,
Vieni meco t'a spetta la bruna
Fida barca del tuo marinar;

Ma tu dormi e non pensi al tuo fido,
Ma non dorme chi vide d'amor!
Io la notte a te vola sul lido
ed il giorno a te volo col cor.

Vieni sul mar,
Vieni a vogar,
Sentirai l'ebbrezza
Del tuo marinar.

Da quel giorno che t'ho conosciuta,
Oh fanciulla di questo mio cuor,
Speme e pace per te ho perduto
Perche` t'amo d'un immenso amor.

Fra le belle tu sei la piu` bela,
Fra le rose tu sei la piu` fin,
Tu del ciel sei brillante stella
Ed in terra sei belta` divin.

Vieni sul mar....

Ah! wake up girl, look at the moon
It casts its rays over the sea,
Come with me, my boat is waiting for you
trust your boat to your sailor.

But you're asleep not thinking of trust
but your lover must wait while you slumber
I fly the night away on the shore
and by day you fly with your heart.

Come to the sea
Come let's row together
You'll feel the gentil breeze,
Together with your mariner.

From that day that I first met you,
Oh dear girl of my heart
I have lost all hope and peace
Because I love you immensely.

Among all the beauties, you are the most beautiful
Among all the roses you are the finest
You're the brightest star of heaven
And here on earth, you're a divine beauty.

Come to the sea....

Vilota di Rovigo

The vilota is an ancient musical form of choral and dance music popular in northern Italy, centered in the Friuli -Veneto region. Vilote are usually short pieces with eight syllables per verse. This vilota is from Rovigo (Veneto).

Strum Pattern: 8

Track 9

Mama mia dame un franco
ca me compra `na capela
co tre metri de cordela
la capela voi portar.

Mama mia dame un franco
ca me compra` `na capela
e si ben ca no son bela
la caplela voi portar

Mama mia dame un franco
ca me compra un fazzoletto
col ricamo e col merleto
col ritrato del mio ben.

Mom can I have a franc
so that I can buy a hat
with three meters of cord
you can wear the hat.

Mom give me a franc
so that I can buy a hat
although its not beautiful
you can wear the hat.

Mom give me a franc
so that I can buy a handkerchief
with embroidery and lace,
and with a portait of my love.

Vurria 'Ca Fosse Ciaola

Villanella alla Napoletana from the 16th century. This Renaissance love song written in the vernacular is one's desire to become a bird so that he can fly into his lover's window to admire her and to be as close as possible.

* Strum and Pick patterns follow the guitar rhythm as indicated.

132

Vurria 'ca fosse ciaola e ca vulasse (2x)
a 'sta fenesta a dirte 'na parola,
ma no ca me mettisse a la gaiola.

E tu da dinto subbeto chiamasse (2x)
viene marotta mia, deh vieni Cola,
ma no ca me metisse a la gaiola.

Et io venesse et hommo ritornasse (2x)
comm'era pimmo e te truvasse sola,
ma no ca me mettisse a la gaiola.

E po' turnasse a lu buon sinno gatta (2x)
ca me n'ascesse pe' la cataratta,
ma che 'na cosa me venesse fatta

The poetry of this villanella is full of renaissance metaphor. The text expresses one's "wish to become"
something from the animal world in order to be close to
the one they love. This was a particularly common form of expressing one's love and admiration
in the 16th century Neapolitan vernacular.
In this villanella, the lover wishes to become a "ciaola", (a magpie or crow) who can fly into the window of
his/her loved one to say a word, as long as he/she is not put into a cage- "ma no ca me metisse a la gaiola".

NOTES

NOTES